AN
EXPERIMENT
IN LEISURE

AN
EXPERIMENT
IN LEISURE

Joanna Field
(Marion Milner)

WITH A FOREWORD BY
GABRIELE LUSSER RICO

JEREMY P. TARCHER, INC.
Los Angeles
Distributed by St. Martin's Press
New York

First published in 1937 by Chatto & Windus
Library of Congress Cataloging in Publication Data
Milner, Marion Blackett.
    An experiment in leisure.

    Originally published: London: Chatto & Windus,
1937. With new foreword.
    1. Leisure—Psychological aspects.   2. Diaries—
Therapeutic use.   3. Introspection.   I. Title.
GV14.4.M46   1987   790'. 0 1'32   87-7138
ISBN 0-87477-453-5

Jeremy P. Tarcher, Inc.
9110 Sunset Blvd.
Los Angeles, CA 90069

Manufactured in the United States of America
10 9 8 7 6 5 4 3 2 1

First Edition

Again
to
D. M.

"All of which, stated simply, in a brief poetic lie, would run: 'I was pleased to see Selina.' That's somehow plain and powerful. A man's statement, carrying one sanguinely along the surface of life that is so plain and simple-oh: 'Tell me, my dear, exactly what you mean, in a few words.' My God!"

Dorothy Richardson

"I found that, taking almost anything as a starting-point and letting my thoughts play about it, there would presently come out of the darkness, in a manner quite inexplicable, some absurd or vivid little incident more or less relevant to that initial nucleus. Little men in canoes upon sunlit oceans would come floating out of nothingness, incubating the eggs of prehistoric monsters unawares; violent conflicts would break out amidst the flower-beds of suburban gardens; I would discover I was peering into remote and mysterious worlds ruled by an order logical indeed but other than our common sanity."

H. G. Wells

CONTENTS

CHAPTER I

CHAPTER II

CHAPTER III

CHAPTER IV

CHAPTER V

CHAPTER VI

xi

CONTENTS

CHAPTER VII

How should the story end, what will hatch from the cocoon, gentleness or fierceness? How to reconcile the opposites of impulse, seeking the magical grip on the lion of desire.   *page* 88

CHAPTER VIII

Finding further terms in which to express my problem from a modern play, 'WITHIN THE GATES'. I suspect that there are other results from the internal action of submission, besides the combating of fear, results connected with the fertility of the mind.   *page* 100

CHAPTER IX

Haunting images from a bull-fight drive me to consider this possibility further.   *page* 111

CHAPTER X

Feeling drives me to study 'PEER GYNT.' Ibsen seems to be saying that true fertility of the mind, true imagination, depends on the willingness to give up all sense of being 'master of the situation'.   *page* 122

CHAPTER XI

What causes the change from imagination as the magic slave of personal desire to imagination as the servant of understanding? Which kind of imagination is religion concerned with?   *page* 131

CONTENTS

CHAPTER XII

CHAPTER XIII

CHAPTER XIV

CHAPTER XV

CONTENTS

CHAPTER XVI

Comparison with other people suggests that there are certain temperaments for whom these problems mean nothing, others for whom they are real. Futility of seeking a way out by trying to copy the 'men of power' and taking arms against the sea.

CHAPTER XVII

How does being a woman affect the problem? Possible reasons why it is harder for a woman to be creative in her understanding as well as in her body.

CHAPTER XVIII

SUMMING UP: Reconciliation of feeling and reason: I have become certain of the need to attend to the voice of the blood and the bones, but not to take it at its face value. I have been forced to conclude that the laws of the imagination are not the same as the laws of action; imagination does not yield to the force of the will, either to destroy its evil or promote its good—but it seems to yield to the wiping out of the will. Alternative Freudian interpretations of this internal gesture of wiping out the will. Use of this illogical gesture to avoid logical pitfalls in thinking, and undue reliance upon authority. Need to relinquish all that has been said.

FOREWORD

Joanna Field's remarkable book, written in 1937, is a compelling account of a psychologist's attempt to use herself as an experimental subject to acknowledge—and value—another way of knowing that counterbalances our logical, linear knowing. Her experiment in leisure, most simply put, is an experiment in "letting go." Such letting go is a way to discover inner images, leading to meaningful patterns that come from within, rather than being imposed from without.

Letting go. Trust. Wonder. Curiosity. These are the necessaries for allowing the inner ear to attune itself to clues of feeling. Without access to this open-ended mode of thought, it is difficult to counteract the "shoulds," "oughts," and "musts" of reason and of "trying harder," which all too often submerge this less-visible thinking process inherent in all of us.

The persistent, insistent outer voice of conventional wisdom tends to see the cause/effect of events, whereas the more delicate inner voice tends to make metaphoric leaps.

As Field began to pay leisurely attention to the unfolding of her inner, spontaneous images, she discovered that she was getting in closer touch not only with the rich inner landscape of her emotions, but also with her outer world; she often made new, unexpected connections. These connections brought a new awareness of recurring patterns in her life. Paradoxically, this simple act—available to all of us—of waiting leisurely for inner images to emerge was hard to learn, harder to allow to happen, and hardest to remember to do. The logical mode of thought, which seeks solutions to problems, reasserted itself whenever she lost her attitude of leisurely observing.

Nevertheless, her experiment eventually paid off: Field learned to escape from logically knowing what ought to be done at the intellectual level but not being able to practice it at a deeper level. She learned that images hold great emotional power and that, unacknowledged and unexpressed, these images remain only vague urgings—but when expressed they become guides to more purposeful, wholesome, "reasonable" living in which emotions can be channeled constructively.

The process she discovered in her experiment is approximate, but decipherable into the following stages:

1. Waiting for clues by moving into an "inner spaceless space" where images from the past or from myth or fairy tales emerge un-

FOREWORD

bidden—they seem to be inexplicably attached to one's personal life, creating a certain resonance.

2. Following those clues of feeling, much as we idly follow a dominant thread in a tapestry, clarifying the resonance.

3. Accepting unknown factors and "holding" them until they become part of an increasingly clear pattern.

4. Watching for the emergence of organic images that create the evolving pattern.

5. Giving the felt pattern expression in line, words, and music; in sum, doing what philosopher Susanne Langer called "giving form to feeling."

The results are mind changes, insights, and sudden new perceptual shifts that illuminate a pattern in one's life to which one might otherwise have been blind. Through her experiment, Field became aware of concentration processes having little to do with logic or with preordained forms. She found that learning to trust this mode of knowing had enormous power to shape her continually shifting sense of identity. *Not* to trust this inner process, she asserts, is "an effective education in self-deception" through involuntarily living one's life according to external rules.

The growing tip of one's life, she discovered, is determined by this inner vision; it depends on a willingness to play with organic images until some sort of meaningful pattern emerges. That moment is the moment of "incipient fruitfulness."

Field made her experiment in leisure in the '30s; her book was published in 1937. Today, much of current brain research confirms her discoveries about two ways of knowing. Her book represents a fascinating story of self-discovery, more relevant today than fifty years ago. It is a story of potential mental powers available to all of us—powers for understanding and channeling the direction of our lives.

E.M. Forster wrote: "only connect"—so simple, yet so impossible unless we discover our innate gift to connect as an integral part of our mental makeup. Field's sensitive and courageous account of her inner voyage of discovery not only fascinates, but also helps you experiment to discover your own inner powers for more creative, more satisfying living.

Gabriele Lusser Rico

INTRODUCTION

THIS book began with an attempt to solve certain aspects of the everyday problem of what to do with one's spare time. Obviously, for a large number of people this is not a problem at all, it is not a problem for those people who are quite sure who and what they are, and who have definite clear-cut opinions about everything. But there are others who are less certain in their attitudes, who are often more aware of other people's identity than their own, and for them I think the problem is real. For them, and very often they are women, it is so fatally easy to live parasitically upon other people's happiness, to answer the question— 'What shall we do today?' by—'We'll do whatever you like, my dear.'

The method of looking for a solution to this problem is a development of one that I had used before; I have tried to find out by simple observation just what this particular mind (I hesitate to call it mine, because during the course of this experiment I came to feel less and less possessive about it) seems to find most interesting. By this I mean that I have followed feeling, the feeling of interest, and tried to find out where it led. Out of this first question of what does one like best grew a second: 'Is this feeling of liking something trustworthy at all, is feeling a safe guide?' I had been driven to ask the second question because for a long time I had suffered from a growing uneasiness over the anti-intellectual trends of modern life. This uneasiness was not entirely disinterested, it grew from the knowledge that I myself had always been more guided by feeling than by reason; although loving the clear precision of science and rational exposition I had always felt it to be slightly foreign and a little dangerous, too clear to be true—and also too difficult for the ordinary business of living. But now I was continually reading accounts of how the uncritical exaltation of feeling seemed to be leading to manifestations which with my whole soul I loathed: to intolerance and ruthless tyranny over individual freedom of thought. Particularly did the distortion of facts for the sake of arousing and exploiting the feelings of the masses make me feel physically sick, as though the ground had fallen away under my feet. I had decided therefore that my experiment with leisure interests might also provide a way for studying certain feelings and might show me under what circumstances they were to be trusted, if at all.

Since I found that it is difficult to compare feelings in the moment of living them I decided to begin by comparing memories, I would go over in my mind some of the things I most liked to think about, not only those memories having the peculiar warm quality that one rather lamely calls 'interest', but also those having that curious un-ease of attraction that being 'in love' brings. I would investigate particularly those ideas that I could not get out of my head, both the pleasant ones and those others that had the fascination of horror—for presumably I liked these too, in a roundabout way, else why should I bother to think about them? I would pick whatever stood out in my memory, not just after each day, as I had tried to do once before, but for the whole of my life, from hobbies, from journeys, from books I had read, plays I had seen, as well as from moments of everyday living.

Of course I knew that such a method would bring to light material that the psycho-analyst would claim was only his to interpret. But as most of us have to learn to reflect upon our lives without a daily hour of help from the psycho-analyst, I did not let this knowledge daunt me. Nor did I try to force psycho-analytic interpretations upon what I observed if the spontaneous wanderings of my mind did not seem to lead me to them. I did, however, borrow one guiding principle from psycho-analysis, the principle that when you give your mind the reins and let it rove freely, there is no such thing as irrelevance, so far as the problems of the mind are concerned, whatever thought pops up is in some way important, however far-fetched it may appear. This principle, based on the truth that the mind has concerns of its own which are not at all identical with one's conscious purposes, I had learnt from psychoanalytic literature and personal experiment. What I had not learnt from the orthodox writings, but my own experience had forced me to admit, was that these private concerns of the mind were not exclusively disreputable, that my mind could be not only stupider and more bestial than I knew, but also wiser. I once heard leisure defined by a psycho-analyst as the process of looking into one's impulses and allowing them. It was also added that many of us have never discovered how to do this, our impulses are so immature that we cannot even admit them to ourselves, much less carry them out in action, so we are not capable of real leisure at all. Certainly I was to find that my deepest impulses were concerned with something so fantastic that at first sight it could not possibly be 'allowed'. But when I had looked into this impulse further I began to guess that it might not be as fantastic as it seemed, I became convinced that my mind knew more of what I was about than I did, like Balaam's ass it could perhaps see the angel of the Lord, but had no adequate language to tell me about it—or rather, it had a language, but one that I had not, until now, bothered to learn.

I had also heard it stated that, the difficulties of mental growth being so great, we all develop some kind of neurosis, but that the secret of happy living is to discover what your own neurosis is, and to learn how to use it.   So perhaps this book could be called a study in the use of masochism; but it is less concerned with names than with a method, and with the attempt to record experience as I saw it.

As for what I have called my discoveries, it will be obvious that they were only new for me, many of them are in fact truths that have been proclaimed at intervals throughout the centuries. But since "axioms in philosophy are not axioms until they have been proved upon our pulses",[1] I have hopes that this account may be of interest to others, not as new truth, but as a method by which an ordinary person can become aware of some of the processes of life that are going on within himself.

[1] Keats.

CHAPTER ONE

WHEN first setting out on this experiment I thought I had better begin with what seemed easiest, so I simply let my mind run back over pleasant memories. As I wanted to see what would come first into my head, I did not attempt any logical order, but just started writing and watched what happened:

. . . Those long hot days when we played tennis and went picnics on bicycles, I suppose I was eighteen and had just found out that I could go about as I liked and when I liked, after all the time-tables and bells of boarding-school life—funny that this should be the first thing I should think of; I suppose I'd suddenly become more aware that I was alive, those first holidays without grown-ups when W. and I bicycled down to the sea, riding across Sussex early on a June morning. But early morning makes me think of that first Cambridge May-week and coming home in the sun after dancing all night—it was that I liked best, the rest was exciting but a bit worrying, I didn't know quite how to deal with all that new world of people—and then all the later holidays we had, getting up by starlight and setting off before dawn with our rucksacks, to get the cool of the day, particularly that morning at Aosta, looking up from the dark street to find the telegraph wires crowded with sleepy swallows just beginning to twitter—that

I

marvellous feeling that rucksack holidays give you: you just set off whenever you want to and stop wherever you find a nice village . . . But suddenly now I've thought of quite different pleasures, the stable things, having tea on a green lawn with big shady trees, and cress sandwiches and those teacups of such delicate china that a dim glow of light came through . . . but now there are such floods of memories I can't write them all, rivers and picnics and dancing and travel and new clothes and old clothes . . . but these are all very simple pleasures—physical ones really—suddenly my memory seems to have changed gear, and I'm remembering another kind, all the people I have known, the excitement of getting to know someone, that day when R. asked me to tea and he'd put pheasant-eyed narcissus and silver willow catkins in his room. But these memories of people are less unalloyed delight than the physical ones. I remember so many misunderstandings, agonies of shyness when I could not get to know people because I liked them too much. . . .

Here I stopped writing, because, wading through such a flood of remembered faces and feelings, I found I had lost sight completely of that sense of allurement which I had decided should be the guide in my search. This, then, was evidently not going to be a good method, I was too overwhelmed by the multiplicity of experience. Perhaps it would be better if I tried to remember something more definite—hobbies, for instance.

With this in mind I thought back to the time when, about eleven or so, I had decided that I would become a professional naturalist. I had read somewhere that the first essential for a naturalist was to keep notes, so I began a Nature Diary and continued to keep it for eight or nine years. Reminded now of those long days of wandering about the countryside, I went to hunt up the old diary and see whether it might perhaps still arouse the old feelings of importance. To my surprise it did ; even the first smudgy page with its drawing of a pair of wild duck gave me a feeling of excitement that seemed out of all proportion to the subject. And there were other drawings, of a sundew plant, and a lace-fly, and nettle-leaved bell flower. I read:

May 18th. Found an early purple orchis and a marsh orchis. Saw a small meadow brown and a fritillary.
27th. Saw a red-backed shrike.
Found a willow wren's nest with six eggs on Holmbury Hill; it was close to the ground under a tuft of heather, dome-shaped and lined with chickens' feathers.

Led by a curious remote sense of intimacy in these scrappy observations, I read further. Gradually, in the second and third year of the diary, when I was thirteen, the notes became more detailed:

Scotland, August 14th. Found the skull of a deer on the moor—with tufts of fur scattered about, two hoofs with part of the legs, splintered bones, and also feathers of grouse. Perhaps the deer was shot, badly wounded, and the men were unable to find it. There were black feathers too, perhaps the ravens, who live quite close on the Pass of Ribhoan, killed a grouse here.
Then I saw a stoat chasing a young rabbit. The rabbit squealed and ran round in circles, scarcely trying to

3

escape the stoat, who followed with long leaps. When the stoat saw me it stopped and sat up. It then glided away into the corn, and the rabbit ran into the wood.

August 20th. I watched a spider take hold of an ordinary house-fly which was alive and had been caught in the web. He started to suck the fly's blood, but before it was quite dead I knocked the spider away; but he rushed back, and seizing it in his black jaws, carried it off, pinching its head.

Saw some dippers; they have a weird little chattering song and it is very difficult to tell where it comes from.

Surrey, September. Found a peewit killed by flying against the telegraph wires.

Also every year I had noted the dates on which the signs of spring appeared; for instance, in the year I was fourteen:

January 1st. Male willow flower out.

29th. Heard the chaffinch, blackbird, thrush, lark, wren and hedge-sparrow sing, though not their full song. Saw a cock blackbird chasing a hen.

February 3rd. Found a peacock butterfly.

24th. Heard the breeding note of a chaffinch.

29th. Heard a greenfinch's note.

March 11th. Cock yellow-hammers still in flocks. Wood violets out.

Then, in the summer of that year, there was a note and a drawing:

FIG. 1.

August 21st. Found an octopus[1] in the mud at low tide.

[1] Actually it was a cuttlefish.

4

CHAPTER ONE

I wondered what on earth there could be in the thought of an octopus in the mud, that could so grip one's heart—but I did not know where to look for a reason. Reading on, I found that now there was more variety in the record, there were notes on the weather, the stars and the countryside, as well as on living things:

August 10th. Saw a great many shooting stars, Jupiter very big and bright in the S.E. at 8 p.m.

11th. Arrowhead and frog-bit and teazles in flower on Pevensey Marshes.

24th. Big wild marshes at Rye with herons.

October 22nd. A large flock of gulls flew over the grounds, flying high towards White Parish Down.

November 13th. Peewits in flocks on the Downs and fields. Heard a linnet singing.

December 5th. Gentian in flower on the Downs, and buttercups and heartsease. Warm wet weather with strong winds, thrushes and robins singing.

26th. Very hard gale. Little birds unable to fly against it and blown about like leaves. Even big oaks sway and quiver in the wind.

28th. Red deadnettle and speedwell out. Starlit nights and cloudy days; leaves of the green-man orchis up.

For January 20th I found the note:

Owls hoot on starlit nights when it is a little bit frosty.

And for February 5th:

Orion is high over the South at 9 o'clock.

AN EXPERIMENT IN LEISURE

And then, not only the bird choruses of spring but the silences of late summer:

> July 27th. Willow wrens are singing in the garden, but no other birds, not even robins. Clear starlit nights and hot still days with all the lavender in flower.

The next year I had discovered new things about the spring:

> April 29th. The wood on the hill is carpeted with primroses, anemones, dog-mercury and cuckoo-flower, and the willows are all golden. No leaves are out, only a purple haze over the woods to show that the buds are swelling. As I stood still on the bank between the wood and the field I could hear little gurglings and bubblings going on all about me, as the hot sun melted the frost out of the ground.

A year later another interest appeared, for we had begun to keep bees and the notes reminded me how their moods had dominated the garden.

> March 6th. . . . little red flowers out on a larch tree by the woodcock wood, and the leaves just showing. The bees are working happily in the willow by the gate, they bring in light and dark yellow pollen.

And then on July 29th:

> . . . The bees swarmed. It was a hot sultry day with a thunderstorm in the evening. They were angry and disturbed all the next day.

Drawings in the following year showed a phase of interest in insects and cold-blooded beasts. I remembered loving the excuse to linger over every detail of their colouring and shape.

6

CHAPTER ONE

Here certainly were many things that I had once found intensely interesting, and they still held my thought with a sense of richness, a remote feeling of life-and-death importance. But the revival of these memories did not seem to be advancing my main problem at all, since it had not told me what I most wanted to do now; to find out about the habits of animals and birds was no longer the pinnacle of enjoyment that it had been in childhood. Also this change fretted me, I felt a little cheated that the observation of wild nature had so lost its glamour. But just what it was I wanted to do instead I could not tell.

Looking over the notes for the year in which I was seventeen I found some new interests developing, and hoped that these might provide some clue. First, there had been thoughts of the healing properties of herbs, and I had made drawings of useful wild flowers to make sure of recognizing them. I found no suggestion in the notes that I ever made any use of these remedies, although it occurs to me now that the names alone could have provided enough reason for the interest—centaury, meadowsweet, vervain, melilot, comfrey, pennyroyal, sanicle, agrimony. And perhaps it was the same motive that led, a year later, to the note that in April I had planted in my garden hyssop, winter savory, tarragon, bergamot, sweet basil, coriander and myrrh ; for I do not remember any use being made of the plants when they came up. After that there had been an interest in natural dyes from plants. I had read somewhere that yellow bedstraw, whose smell took me back to long August days by the sea, would produce

7

a deep red, while blue could be simmered out from the root of that yellow iris which had been the day's spoil from so many childhood river picnics. As for yellow, it would come from infusions of gorse, bracken, broom, agrimony, St. John's wort, sundew, kingcups—names every one of which was the key to some memory. So I had hopefully collected barks and roots and flowers and simmered them over the kitchen fire, once even succeeding in dyeing enough stuff to make myself a blouse.

Reading through the notes, I found I could still bask in the power these things held in my memory—but I also felt there was something I did not understand about them. I was particularly puzzled when I compared them with memories of people. For during those years I had been involved in the usual childish love-affairs, all of which had had a desperate importance at the time, but now seemed so remote that I could hardly believe they had occurred. I had even kept a spasmodic diary of my daily occupations, including brief notes on my human loves, but these had no power to stir me now, they only seemed self-conscious and rather futile. Of course, there had also been other kinds of pleasure in relationships with people, I had been lucky in having many companions of my own age and I had found a deep, steady satisfaction in them. But it had been a satisfaction I took for granted. It was quite apart both from the spasmodic falling in love with older people, or from the private delight in observing the changes of nature. In fact, in some curious way I seemed to have lived more intensely in the outer world of nature than in my own life of loves and hates and daily happenings. So, when at fifteen I went to boarding school in the summer term, I had not felt I was living at all except on those few days when there were picnics or when I managed to escape from games and roam the Downs. It was not that I had not, on the whole, thoroughly enjoyed the games and the school life, it was only that it had not seemed real; real life, the business that I ought to be getting on with, was out in the fields. I remembered sitting at French lessons gazing through the window at the dim line of woods that cloaked the Downs, so deeply longing to be there that my whole body ached with it.

In order to find some hint of the reason for this gap I now thought I would try looking for memories from the period before I began to keep a Nature Diary.

For a long time I was haunted by a feeling of richness in these early years, as if I had then been in touch with something that, in a minute or two, I would remember all about. I now thought that if I methodically put down all that had happened, as far as I could remember it, I must surely discover what it was that had been so lovely. But I was to be disappointed, the more I wrote the more the glamour faded; memories grew barer and barer, more and more trivial, till finally interest only remained in the everyday sensory things that I did not think were easy to write about, the memories of smells and the feeling of air, warmth and coolness, cool bare knees, hot sand. Then it occurred to me that perhaps I was being too deliberate in my efforts, trying to remember systematically and give a coherent account of what had happened, rather than letting the mind speak for itself. So I tried again, this time letting the memories come haphazard, just as I had done, but perhaps with too little persistence, at the outset of my experiment:

'When I was six, those little white round cherry buds in the cherry walk, the pond it led to, all white with water-crowfoot; the cinder path by the railway with poppies; sundews on the damp parts of the heath, and the new grass after heath fires; that hot sandy path and making little bows and arrows; the young oak-leaves and standing on the smooth stones in the stream, barefoot. Buying pansies and violas off a market cart for my garden; little green moths coming out of the nut bushes in the cool evening; making clay beads and painting them.'

This was better, the delight still remained in each image as I remembered it; yet they were such everyday things, simple, sensory pleasures; it was difficult to account for their sense of world-shattering importance. And I did not feel content after writing them down, the impulse to take hold of something from memory had not been satisfied. Suddenly I broke off writing such memories and made a note:

'So little to write, so rich to feel; what is it that I want to remember?' And immediately another trivial image filled my mind: 'Thrush singing, eggs in the nest, I'd watched it building; blackbird's nest in the holly bush with wool in it. . . .' Here I stopped. Surely it could not be important to remember every nest I had found? The red wool, I remembered, had amused me (I was twelve or thirteen then), because the blackbird had evidently used the sweepings off our dining-room carpet as nest material. But why on earth should this be important to remember? Then it occurred to me that I might give up effort still further; I could stop directing my thoughts even towards the facts of childhood, simply let images flow as they would, present or past, fact or phantasy. And since I had stopped on the memory of this red wool in the blackbird's nest I thought I might just as well take that as my starting place:

'Red wool, red weaving, raiment, "all glorious within", riches, jewels, box of treasure, hidden, pirate treasure, we made a desert island map to show where it was hidden, gold, "gold and silver will not do, my fair lady", fair, beautiful, gold and silver, "picking up gold and silver", daisies, white and gold, smell of lawns smooth mown, evenings, setting sun coming in through the chink in the blinds, gold and silver, silver, silver spoon, Christmas trees, still the rich gold feeling, Field of the Cloth of Gold, woven, curtain in the Temple, blue and purple and scarlet—blue. . . .'

Then with a sudden reversal of mood "the rich gold feeling" vanished, and other images flowed in:

'. . . blue, blue with cold, blue nose, nipped, "blackbird nipped off her nose", nose, nosey Parker, "Dong with the luminous nose", nose, our dog who smelt out a nest in the wood, I was only three, wood, dark, ivy, woods, damp, still, high-up chirp of little birds, hanging grey lichen in that Scotch forest, the still dark wood in Dovedale, I found enchanter's nightshade there, damp black earth, rich, the river below, my father fishing,

fishing at Sea-houses off the harbour, sandhills, sand-hills, Beadnell, beads, St. Cuthbert's beads, which were little fossil worms, that upheaved rock, fires tearing and rending the earth, upheavals . . .!! NOW I'VE GOT IT.'

FIRES TEARING AND RENDING THE EARTH, UPHEAVALS. . . .

In a flash I was sure that this was what I had been looking for. In my attempt to reconstruct the memories of childhood, objectively, I had for instance written:

'The photo I took when I was 12, of that curious rock on the coast at Dunstanborough. I stuck it in my Nature Diary and also sent it in to the holiday photography exhibition. The early rock strata had been thrown up in a curious contorted curve by some volcanic eruption.'

To the objective mind this incident marked a growing conscious interest in science. But now I suddenly guessed that to another part of the mind it meant something else. Just as I had once before discovered that I had two quite different groups of ideas about God,[1] according to whether I thought deliberately, or simply let thoughts come of their own accord, so this rock had two different meanings. To part of my mind it was an interesting geological specimen, to the other it stood now for the idea of hidden inner fires, powerful and un-accountable, upheaving and rending the surface. The first meaning had left me bored and depressed at the futility of what I was writing, the second had given me

[1] *A Life of One's Own*, J. P. Tarcher, Inc.

such deep satisfaction that I knew it was one of those significant memories from childhood that my questing imagination had been groping after.

But though my feelings told me this was what I wanted to remember, they did not explain why such an idea should be important. Why should the idea of the inner fires of the earth have shattering importance, either to a twelve-year-old—or to me as I looked back on that twelve-year-old—since it was quite possible that I was reading my own present sense of its importance into my memory of that experience? Volcanic eruption was not likely to be an important part of my life then, or now. I thought that the only answer could be that it was important by analogy, that the idea of the inner fires of the earth was sufficiently like some other experience to be able to stand for, or symbolize, some experience that was too dimly felt or too complex and obscure to be expressed more directly. I wondered, did this possibly throw some light on my early passionate interest in nature? I had a long way to go before I could see the connection, but I felt sure the connection was there. My next clues actually emerged from a study of journeys.

CHAPTER TWO

It had often puzzled me how those glimpses of people or scenery that were particularly impressive when travelling were so difficult to communicate. And yet I had an aching desire to—feeling, I think, that if only my friends could be made to realize and share my experience I would somehow possess it more surely. At one time I collected picture post cards, hoping that by them I could recapture and explain the power of those glimpses. But I never managed to. Politely my friends looked at the post cards, but hurriedly, not realizing at all, I felt, what it had meant to me to be there. Then also that curious sense of importance that having been to places brings; was it merely to impress my friends or to get an inner expanded feeling, that I would say unconcernedly, as I have caught myself doing —"Oh yes, I saw that in New York"? I began to think that it could not be entirely in order to feel " one up " on other people that one so cherished the thought of one's travels, and that seeing new sights did something more than satisfy idle curiosity. But just what was the cause of this extreme fascination of foreign countries, especially the first glimpses of them? Why should strangeness in itself be so intensely alluring—or rather, not all strangeness, but only certain particular moments?

To answer this question I decided to go over in my

14

mind all the things I had seen which had gripped my heart with such a curious strength. Not all of them were in themselves impressive sights, in fact many of the acknowledged impressive ones, like the New York sky-line first seen from the harbour, did not have this intimate, gripping quality—rather, for me, the view from Manhattan across the Hudson to where the plateau of New Jersey ended in a sheer drop to the river was far more important. Day after day, during my first weeks in America, I had stared across and seen that flat top of the cliff but nothing beyond it, waiting for the spring when I should set out to explore a whole new continent. And then:

'. . . the whistling call of the joncos in the bare trees of those New York City parks, and the thought of a whole continent of strange birds.

'. . . that trip to Virginia in the hushed warmth of the Indian summer, and how, on a picnic, someone pointed out the old slave quarters in a farm we were passing.

'. . . driving due south from Chicago in the first hot days of Spring, after those bitter sleet storms in Canada, how the first night out from Chicago we turned off the road to camp in a little wood—and, after a whole day of rattling along the high road, found ourselves in a sudden stillness that was alive with continual flutterings and twitterings and snatches of bird-songs—those flashes of colour, a continual coming and going through the branches that were only just beginning to show a mist of green—cardinals, bluebirds, mocking birds, surely there were all these—and that lovely little red-headed woodpecker.

'. . . driving across Missouri, heading for the Pacific, that night out from St. Louis, when the darkness of the wood we camped in was suddenly full of dancing stars, and we wondered if it was the fault of the sardines we'd eaten—till we remembered fireflies.

'. . . that sleepy village we drove through in the hot afternoon, the men sitting on rocking-chairs smoking and dozing—and then we read that this same village lynched a negro.

'. . . those first warm nights of the southern spring, suddenly hearing a voice out of the still, velvety blackness, a little negro boy who had come to beg, but I could see nothing of him because he matched the night.

'. . . driving in a cloud of red dust, which one morning changed to white, as we crossed a State border, and the horizon was filled with white cone-shaped hills—a mining country—and the flat dry fields between the hills smouldering with a flame-coloured flower.

'. . . those hot dusty days of continual rattle and bump, hoping to bathe, but the rivers looked so sluggish and thick with mud. That day I could bear it no longer and slipped down from the road to where a little muddy river ran hidden by leaves—standing naked on the water's edge in the flickering gloom, trying to wash the red dust out of my hair—but just as I splashed the cool water over me, hearing the rustle of someone moving in the bushes on the far bank, so that my bathe was spoilt.

'. . . then at last, crossing a quick-flowing river with boulders and clear water, and running down to it joy-

16

fully, only to find every stone rimmed with a shining brown scum of greasy oil, and the air reeking with it.

'. . . later that same day, the sudden view of oil-derricks, covering the country like forests of blasted pine trees—and everywhere the hot smell of tarry oil.

'. . . crossing into the State of Oklahoma, with the thermometer at 90°, that great river we came upon; how, from a distance we had seen white beaches, and then, panting for coolness, had jumped out of the car and stripped on the smooth sand—but climbing out on a log to dive, we remembered first to test the depth—and found it barely knee-deep! And how, venturing farther, we found we could paddle right across it, although the river-bed was five times as wide as the Thames at Richmond. And that was coming near to the part of the country where all the summer the rivers were nothing but rivers of smooth white sand—but we did not know that then . . . Coming back to dress, the sudden stop at seeing a huge black snake, seeing it writhe across our camping ground, the first we had seen in America, how sinister and enormous it seemed—and afterwards, resting cautiously through the heat of that day, always expecting snakes, and drinking tepid purple grape juice, till the ants discovered it and climbed in to drown themselves in hundreds—then in the evening, which did not bring any coolness with it, setting out again, noticing a cactus by the roadside, and the boom of distant thunder. How dark it got, but too quickly and heavily for evening, and when we drove down a side-road to camp for the night the sultriness had changed to a fierce hot wind, which roared as it bent young saplings nearly to the ground, amid a scud of stripped-off leaves. How we wondered, did hurricanes or tornadoes begin like this? Would the car be blown over? Ought we to get out and shelter in that little gully of red sandstone? In the false darkness hills showed dark purple and the sheet lightning was a purple glare lighting up the red earth, purple like the grape juice in which the ants had drowned themselves.

' . . . visits to the Indian pueblos of the Rio Grande, watching a spring festival dance of women, led by that one woman impersonating a goddess; how she made curious slow, rhythmic, growing movements with her hands, while the rest chanted monotonously—prayers for fertility, they said, which depended on rain. And then driving home across the arid waste of sage brush; that wind from the highest mountain slopes bringing the smell of a shower. And how they said there was sweet grass on the higher slopes.

'. . . driving through the night to avoid the Arizona sun—and knowing that away on our left was Meteor City, grown up, they said, to mine the wealth of a great meteorite that had fallen in Indian days. (We never saw it, but it remained more vividly in my mind than many of the cities we did pass through.)

'. . . more long hot days of driving, thunder every afternoon, empty rivers of dry white sand, and those transparent pillars of sand, little whirlwinds that moved over the country ahead of us like Moses's pillar of cloud —or sometimes scudded giddily over the dead river-beds like pale tubular ghosts.

'. . . and then the Grand Canyon. I suppose it was

18

too vast to be absorbed in one impression; I cannot believe I have looked giddily across that great gash in the earth, or walked down it at dawn and paddled in the gloomy Colorado river, the water so thick with swirling sand that they say if you should fall in you would surely drown from the weight of sand in your clothes. My mind will not dare to remember, it is as if someone else were telling me about it.

'. . . dead cattle on the roadside, dead from drought, they said, sometimes only the bare ribs sticking up, sometimes the whole rotting carcass.

'. . . driving by night across the Mojave desert because of the heat, and, stopping to change a punctured tyre in the dead inky stillness, seeing something move on the sand in the ring of my electric torch, and knowing it must be a scorpion.

'. . . the freshness that came with that dawn in the desert.

'. . . the first damp wind from the Pacific which met us full in the face when we topped the San Bernardino ridge, and my body sucked up the comfort of it like a thirsty garden.

'. . . and then driving eastward again in the early autumn, the roadside bright with yellow sunflowers. That day when we became aware of small cavalcades emerging from every side on to the plain where our main Santa Fé trail ran, emerging from the distant veil of forest on the mountain slopes, emerging from the valleys, some in covered wagons, some on horseback, some in ancient Fords. And how we found they were all converging on our road and going the same way as we were. And how when they came close we saw they were Navajo Indians, whole families of them, the women stately in tight velvet bodices and bright flowing skirts like Victorian fashions, with silver and turquoise necklaces and earrings. Some were riding on horseback, some in the wagons with their babies. And the men, handsome and silent, with wide cowboy hats and turquoise earrings and silver spurs, each riding as if he made one creature with his horse. And how we found we were all going to that pueblo, Laguna, and they camped there on the hillside, waiting for the fiesta. And all next day the beat of the drum and the continuous chant—was it a rain-dance?—with the silent Navajos sitting round in hundreds, silently watching.

'Then driving on, always eastwards, farther and farther away from the soft life of California, with a growing sense of something looming in the north and closing down on us, the hint of it coming more and more often in the smell of the wind—snow.'

The same thing struck me here as in the Nature Diary. Why was it that all these memories, which were marked with such a peculiar feeling of importance, should again be almost exclusively concerned with natural surroundings, not with people at all, except for Indians? If I had been asked what had interested me most in America, I would have spoken of the people, the people I met and the many different aspects of the social life. But when I asked myself, not my opinions, but my feelings, the answer seemed to be quite different.

In search of further facts to explain this, I decided to let my fancy roam over other journeys. Immediately

CHAPTER TWO

I found myself thinking of a special object of sight-seeing that, ever since my childhood, I had found irresistible—prehistoric stones. I remembered being taken to Stonehenge at about fifteen, and how the image of it had dogged my memory afterwards.

'. . . that first time I saw Stonehenge—and thought it smelt of human sacrifice, felt it as evil yet somehow alluring—and years later, Dartmoor—walking over the moor and suddenly coming upon that Stone Age village, Grim's Pound, the site so well chosen for sun and shelter —and then those stone circles, Grey Wethers they call one of them, close to Bellever Tor—what a name, Bellever—echoes of Baal and the priests of Baal—and then the stone coffins on the hill-tops, Kist Vaens I was told they were—and then the Dolmens in Guernsey, how they haunted me the whole time I was there—and that carved stone goddess which is now a church gate post at St. Martins—they say until quite recently the villagers there crept out at night to lay bunches of flowers before her—and the Rollright stones on the Cotswolds, which they say can never be counted—and the Five Knights stones that are said to troop down to the water on Midsummer night—and those flint arrowheads I was always looking for.'

Why did I find these things so important? My whole body ached with impatience that so little was known about them, and my pilgrimages to such remains always ended in disappointment—merely a few stones —and it was not any good reconstructing in imagination the purposes they were used for. I wanted to know, not to imagine.

AN EXPERIMENT IN LEISURE

And then I went to the Roman villa at Chedworth. In general I had thought the idea of Roman remains dull; they had not the gripping quality of the more primitive. But I found that this villa was different.

'. . . what a feeling they had for a beautiful spot, building their country house at the head of this wide wooded valley with its clear stream, and building it with such wide terraces. So they were not only concerned with soldiers and laws and those terribly purposive roads, as I used to think. Now I can feel them as human beings. That portable stone altar to a goddess; and up in the depth of the woods, they said there was a ruined temple—a pagan worship dominating the whole valley.'

Then also Wychwood Forest in the Cotswolds, I had lived for months where I could see it mistily cloaking the hills across the valley. For me it hung like a dark presence over the whole countryside. For others, too, perhaps, for look at the names of the villages—Shipton under Wychwood, Milton under Wychwood, Ascot under Wychwood. At first I knew nothing of its history; only from the map I saw that there were prehistoric remains within it—Long Barrows. Later I read that it had been a last stronghold of pagan rites in England, and finally I went across the valley to see it. But again, as always in such pilgrimages, I was vaguely disappointed and thwarted; I saw nothing to grip my imagination as the distant view of it had done—except some old twisted thorns. For I had not yet learnt that this strange gripping power that drew me to ancient places did not belong to the thing in itself, but was only a clue pointing further. I remembered the same thing happening on Dartmoor, for I had heard of Wistman's Wood, a grove of ancient trees in the heart of the moor, all gnarled and stunted with age, and I had been deeply pulled to see it, but it was too far to reach on foot from Bellever and the Grey Wethers stones. When years later I made a special expedition to it, I was utterly disappointed, seeing only some very ordinary, small and badly grown oaks.

One day I found that the thread of allurement to places had become entangled with ideas that I remembered from books. Once, when far from thoughts of exploring the countryside, lying in bed after the birth of my son, I found I was repeating the name of a book of short stories that I had just read: *The Runagates Club*.[1] It was so persistent that finally I let go all my absorption with immediate purposes and simply watched my thoughts; as I did so a vague fear grew round the name, and with it the memory of a passage in another book that I had just been reading:

> "It rasped her, though, to have stirring about in her this brutal monster! to hear twigs cracking and feel hooves planted down in the depths of that leaf-encumbered forest, the soul; never to be content quite, or quite secure, for at any moment the brute would be stirring, this hatred . . ."[2]

and then my thoughts jumped to a rough sketch I had myself made at the Zoo (Fig. 2). Spontaneously this thought with its vague fear took the name of "the Green Wildebeste". So that was what the name "Run-

---

[1] John Buchan.   [2] *Mrs. Dalloway*, by Virginia Woolf.

agates Club" had meant to me, for one of the stories in the book, as I remembered it, had been about a curious sanctuary to this selfsame green beast which had supernatural powers. But why was the idea of such a fantastic beast so interesting?

Also in this same book was the story of a ruined Roman temple in the Cotswold woods; it told of how some antiquarian had unearthed an old ritual for invoking the god and then himself became destroyed in a mysterious fire that had its heart in the temple altar. With this thought came the memory of how, a week before, when the pains of labour were beginning, I had at first been rather frightened, but had then plunged deliberately into a lower darker level of awareness, dimly feeling myself part of a dark swirling current, sinking down into my body, with half thoughts of dark earth and bursting seeds, the bark of trees, the strains of rising sap. I had gone to sleep thinking of the hot smell of mud by the river where cows have trodden, muddy water seeping into each hoof-mark, and the smell of trampled reeds. With the next spasm of pain had come the smell of wet charlock fields, deep lanes in chalk country, wet fields and beeches on the Downs blown with a wet wind. Incidentally, I thought it curious that at this time it was imagined smells that became absorbing, whereas at ordinary times I found the memory of smells very hard to recall.

Then on the first warm summer day of that year when back in the country again, I was walking across a marshy buttercup field, and suddenly found myself standing quite still and staring at a cow's hoof-mark sunk deep in the warm earth. I thought: 'Whatever does that remind me of?' for it stirred such a flood of unnamed memories. But I passed on again, uncomprehending.

Later, when I thought over this incident, I remembered certain other ideas that were definitely connected with it, but I could not at first see any reason for the connection. I remembered how in childhood, one of my greatest delights had been certain places by the River Wey where the cows came down to drink, and where, by venturing through the reeds with the warm mud welling up between your toes, you could sometimes pick yellow irises. Later, after some reading of mythology, a dim idea of Pan had become connected with all such river-bank places. Then, after fifteen years, when I had thought it amusing to draw a sort of pictorial map of my life-experience, I had felt impelled to put a pair of great horns as a background against the sky. Now I also remembered how I had sometimes been taken to see demonstrations of English folk-dancing, and one day I had seen a dance which had haunted me for years. It was called "The Horn Dance of Abbots Bromley" and the dancers advanced in slow single file, each carrying a pair of great antlers held above his forehead.

Certainly the theme of horns and hoofs seemed to be cropping up rather frequently. But I could not see any reason for this, so I went on following up the clues of interest.

CHAPTER THREE

FOR a long time I had had a vague interest in witch-craft. This had grown stronger during the months that I had lived with the perpetual presence of Wychwood Forest across the valley, and whenever I heard of a book on the subject I had made a note of it. For some curious reason, however, I never seemed able to bring myself to settle down to read one of these books. Vaguely, I believe, I felt that they would surely not tell me what I really wanted to know, for I had long become used to titles having a glamour that faded as soon as I began to read. As a child I had been given *A Book of Discovery*, a popular history of the great explorers. It was full of beautifully coloured ancient maps and drawings of old sailing ships and I loved to see it in my bookshelf. But I never read more than the first few chapters. It seemed that the details of geographical exploring did not concern me very deeply. In the end it was the same with birds. From the age of ten to fifteen I had read every book about birds I could lay my hands on, and had spent nearly all my spare time watching birds and trying to understand their habits. But later, when I had discovered that actual scientific studies were being made of their capacities and behaviour, I found I could not read the books; it seemed that to know about birds intellectually was not now

26

what I wanted. I wanted to get closer to them than that, I wanted somehow to enter into the vividness of their curious, wayward life, not study it as a thing apart. It was the busy flutter of wings and twitter in tree-tops that I loved most, or the hurried importance of starlings on the lawn, or of a wren collecting nest materials. And it was the same with witchcraft, documents and historic details were apparently not what I wanted. But what it was I did want continued to elude me, until, one day, in a second-hand shop, I happened on a book about witchcraft called *The History of the Devil*.[1]

Up to this time all that I knew about witchcraft had suggested that it was a malevolent thing, an underhand way of getting even with your enemies, or of thinking that you could. But this book emphasized a different aspect, it suggested that popular views of witchcraft were based only on decadent survivals, distorted by ignorant imaginations, of what had once been a deeply serious pagan ritual and belief. Also I had never before thought of connecting witchcraft rites with fertility; but I now remembered how I had years ago been struck by a similarity between the conventional picture of the Devil with horns, hoofs and a tail, and the Greek idea of Pan, great god of flocks and shepherds. Moreover, here in this book I found put forward the idea that those dark ceremonies in the depths of the forest which had so allured me, were the central mysteries of an older religion, that the god they worshipped was not really a personification of evil, but the best symbol they

[1]*History of the Devil*, R. L. Thompson, AMS Press Inc.

knew for the forces of life. Apparently the symbol had only come to be looked upon as evil through contrast with a more mature idea of good; Pan only became the Devil because of the growing idea that the fatness of the land, many children, many flocks, might not satisfy all of man's desires.

I was not, of course, concerned with whether this view corresponded with historical fact, but only with the particular images it suggested. The idea of a bitter war between the old gods and the new was familiar enough; in childhood I had been entranced by the Norse myths of the struggle between the giants and the gods of Valhalla. But what was it that the idea of the worship of the older gods was now drawing me on to discover? In *The History of the Devil* it was suggested that the horns and tail of Pan and the Devil originally came from the hunting-magic ceremonies of cave-men, when the priest-magician disguised himself as an animal, just as in some of the American-Indian dances of to-day. But what had this got to do with me? Thinking it over, I began to see the theme of the horned beast and the horned god cropping up everywhere in my life. I remembered how, in adolescence, I had made little surreptitious flower offerings to Pan, even under the shadow of the ceremonies of the Church of England. Later I had found myself often going to the Zoo to draw animals and had always ended by trying to draw the horned creatures on the Mappin Terraces. Then had come the fear of the horned beast in the Green Wildebeste story, and the fascination of that solemn procession of men in the Horn Dance of Abbots Bromley. It

seemed uncanny the way clue after clue fitted in.   I
even found my Horn Dance mentioned in this same history of the devil.   And there had I been thinking all
this time that my interest in it was one of those wayward
and haphazard enthusiasms, just as pointless and eccen-
tric as loving to draw pictures of goats.

FIG. 2.

But was it really possible that all these curious spasmodic interests could be connected?   Looking back on
my holidays I found many more pieces to fit into the
picture.   Once on someone's mantelpiece I had seen a
little goat, so beautifully carved in wood that when I
went to Switzerland I hunted town after town, hoping
to find the man who had made it.   Then goatherds
with their flocks had always entranced me, once I had
brought back from the mountains of Savoy a goatherd's

29

wineskin—though I found it had such a vile smell, I could never use it to drink from. But granted so many interests pointed in the same direction, what was there at the end of the road? Pan, the Devil, the elder gods, fertility rites, dark ceremonies in forests—and what was I to do about it? The implications seemed a little awkward. Was I to hunt for a present-day company of devil-worshippers and join their ranks? But I knew by the sense of intimacy in all these ideas that it was not a matter to be put lightly aside; if I had set out determined to find the meaning of what was most interesting, then I must face this question. And now all those most vivid memories of the journey across America also flashed into my mind, this time with other associations:

'. . . that view across to the New Jersey cliffs—a story of Conan Doyle's called *The Lost World*—they found a whole world of living prehistoric beasts, cut off from destroying influences because the tableland was surrounded by inaccessible cliffs—what is there interesting about a lost world of animals from the past, great lumbering primitive things?—those slave quarters in Virginia—a negro boy in the dark—darkness—the Moorish look of a horse's collar in Provence—darkness—cave-dwellers—hidden riches in the earth—those mines in Kansas, or was it Oklahoma?—that flame-like flower, strayed somehow from the inner fires of the earth—forests of oil-derricks, how they seemed to blast the countryside—riches in the earth, but also destruction—a land laid waste by boiling lava, that belt of lava in the Rockies where nothing grew, grey black rock—that snake was black, a streak of darkness amongst the lovely sun and grass—and those dead cattle—dis—*dis*-solution, *dis*-solute, *dis*-integrate—but those dark, beautiful people who emerged from all the mountain valleys and slowly converged, all coming together, and next day the quick beat of the drum and the continual dance, all intent upon one thing, before the shrine of green corn.'

But what had I to do with dark powers of the earth in my sober everyday existence? Was all this perhaps only a roundabout way of being preoccupied with physical sex experience, as I thought Freud would say? Was it simply an overflowing of sex energy till it gave its iridescent glow to all my spontaneous interests? And if I could have ten babies, would all this stop? The theme had certainly filled my mind most intensely during the weeks after child-birth. And yet I did not think it was entirely explained by physical sex, although it had certainly to do with relations to people—and to myself. I thought this because one day I experienced a particular contact of minds, or of personality, I do not know what to call it, but it gave me many clues:

'After the misery of the week-end I came to see you, submerged and hoping nothing, only able to keep from tears by the thought that perhaps I could get drunk and see what that was like. But as I came into the room and saw you standing there, waiting, facing me across the room, the air was charged, no more flat and stale. I'd come empty, expecting nothing—is that why you were able to fill me? And afterwards—I certainly walked on air, but it was glowing air and my feet burnished and winged. And this morning I thought it would have gone, but it hasn't, I'm still possessed by

you, myself is only a shell, the living thing in it is you.
I'm an empty shell filled with the sound of the sea,
brimming with it. Is this the losing of oneself, the self-
forgetfulness that so many hunt after? My blood is not
mine, it is a gloriously alive thing, something with purposes not mine, that may even destroy me. But I'm
glad. Once I was revolted at the ichneumon fly grub
that ate its way through the living caterpillar's body, an
alien thing taking its pleasure recklessly. But now I'm
glad, glad to be possessed, possessed by something that
has no consideration for my good. I feel exultant because my good has been wiped out, for I was utterly
tired of striving for my own good. Why should I
approve of you or admire you? What have my little
preferences or ideas got to do with it? I have been
utterly subdued, wiped out, the caterpillar body gone,
eaten away, to serve the purpose of another life, not
even to reproduce its own kind, but an utterly alien
life. . . . And tomorrow I suppose I must meet you
again and talk business and disagree.'

Suddenly I thought I knew what witchcraft had
meant to me. It was obvious that one had a deep
instinct to submit oneself to the best one knew, an
insatiable instinct to adore which would find heroes by
hook or by crook, often making one build fantasies
round people who could never bear such a weight of
the ideal. But here was something else, a darker instinct; for to worship what one thought to be "the
good" was only half the picture. It could not bring
complete submission, for there was still some of one's
own will left in the choice of "the good". I felt:

'If you submit yourself to your idea of God, that's not the ultimate submission, for what about the Devil? Of course, there were those old practices of sacred prostitution and the myths of gods who loved a mortal woman; surely those expressed the truth of the universal female desire to be possessed by the best one knows—that was all right in a less moral age when your god had not yet become the embodiment of goodness, when he was still liable to fierceness. But when man's conscience had so far developed that his god became a god of goodness and paternal love, then submission to the idea of Him lacked the completeness of surrender, for it meant shutting out evil, and therefore still being afraid of it. To submit yourself to an alien force that wishes to destroy you, this seems the only ultimate security.'

I did not put all this down as an argument in theology, but only as an attempt to find a way of expressing feelings that I was dimly aware of as having an overwhelming force. I could not doubt the existence of this feeling, but I had to ask myself what it might mean. This satisfaction in a momentary utter destruction of one's sense of self by an alien force, the final breaking of one's will, was this morbid? I knew to many people it must seem so, yet in every bone in my body I was certain it was not. It would seem morbid at first sight because so much of our accepted ways of living and thinking emphasize the opposing tendency, the desire to assert one's will and make the ego safe. And yet, I thought, the desire to suffer and to find the ultimate destruction of one's own good crops up everywhere in all kinds of self-imposed penances and obligations. When does an impulse that is almost universal cease to become natural and become morbid? I could not tell, but one day I read, in reference to recent views on the desire to inflict pain, and the desire to endure it:

> "To brand as perversions these two inescapable human desires which are implanted in every human being, without exception, and which belong to his nature just as much as his skin and hair, was the colossal stupidity of a learned man. That it was repeated is intelligible. For thousands of years man has been educated in hypocrisy, and it has become a second nature to him. . . . Everyone by reason of his nature must wish to give and to suffer pain; to that he is impelled by Eros." [1]

Yet undoubtedly the desire for pain and self-destruction, if not in itself morbid, did very often express itself in morbid forms, in ways that brought no ultimate happiness or good to anyone, in futile self-abnegations and miseries. I knew people who persistently chose to do the thing that would bring them most pain and who could never accept happiness unreservedly when it came. And surely this question was most relevant to my problem of how to spend my leisure. If this desire to sacrifice my own wants was so strong, I was faced with the paradox that perhaps what I wanted most to do was not to do what I most wanted to do. I knew many people of whom this seemed true, as soon as they had a moment to themselves free from obligations, they would rush off to find another obligation, someone else or something else to sacrifice their lives to.

[1] *The Book of IT*, Georg Groddeck, International Universities Press, Inc.

CHAPTER THREE

Was this morbid? I could not tell, but certainly I noticed that these same people very often had recurrent periods of physical illness when they were forced to attend to themselves, to "mind their own business".

I could hardly avoid the conclusion that this was what all my years of interest in dark pagan ceremonial had been leading up to, for after having been driven, with such pains, to bring these feelings into words, I found myself no longer interested in witchcraft. At the Witches' Sabbath, so said my history of the Devil, the devotees of the cult, in a wild pagan orgy, submitted themselves sexually to the Horned God, or rather to the priestly wizard who represented him. This fact now no longer interested me in any particular way, except historically, as perhaps the final survival of the holy fertility rites of ancient times. Also, incidentally, I found I no longer wanted to draw pictures of the horned beasts on the Mappin Terraces.

CHAPTER FOUR

THIS method of following up whatever ideas held my attention had certainly brought me to some surprising conclusions. I began to realize once more that the business of finding out what sort of thing one likes best is no easy task. For I had been driven to face the possibility that one could actually want to submit to an apparently destroying force, and now there was no going back on this thought, however dark the regions it seemed likely to lead me into.

The theme of witchcraft had now faded from my interests, but there was another connected with pagan ritual that still held my imagination with recurring insistence: the ceremony of the killing of the god. As usual, I had continually evaded coming to grips with the problem. Twelve years before, the theme melody of the impending doom of the gods from *The Ring* had haunted me for weeks; later I was always borrowing Frazer's Golden Bough, but daunted perhaps by its size, I never managed to read it. Then one day, when I happened on a shilling reprint of the Adonis chapter, I bought and devoured it. I read:

"Under the names of Osiris, Tammuz, Adonis, and Attis, the peoples of Egypt and Western Asia represented the yearly decay and revival of life, especially of vegetable life, which they personified as a god who annually died and rose again from the dead. In name and detail the rites varied from place to place: in substance they were the same. . . .

"If a custom of putting a king or his son to death in the character of a god has left small traces of itself in Cyprus, an island where the fierce zeal of Semitic religion was early tempered by Greek humanity, the vestiges of that gloomy rite are clearer in Phoenicia itself and in the Phoenician colonies, which lay more remote from the highways of Grecian commerce. We know that the Semites were in the habit of sacrificing some of their children, generally the first-born, either as a tribute regularly due to the deity or to appease his anger in seasons of public danger and calamity. If commoners did so, is it likely that kings, with all their heavy responsibilities, could exempt themselves from this dreadful sacrifice for the fatherland? In point of fact, history informs us that kings steeled themselves to do as others did. It deserves to be noticed that if Mesha, king of Moab, who sacrificed his eldest son by fire, claimed to be a son of his god, he would no doubt transmit his divinity to his offspring; and further, that the same sacrifice is said to have been performed in the same way by the divine founder of Byblus, the great seat of the worship of Adonis. This suggests that the human representatives of Adonis formerly perished in the flames. At all events, a custom of periodically burning the chief god of the city in effigy appears to have prevailed at Tyre and in the Tyrian colonies down to a late time, and the effigy may well have been a later substitute for a man. For Melcarth, the great god of Tyre, was identified by the Greeks with Hercules, who is said to have burned himself to death on a great pyre, ascending up to heaven in a cloud and a peal of thunder. . . .

AN EXPERIMENT IN LEISURE

"On many a beach and headland of the Aegean, where the Phoenicians had their trading factories, the Greeks may have watched the bale-fires of Melcarth blazing in the darkness of night, and have learned with wonder that the strange foreign folk were burning their god." [1]

I read further that at Gades, the modern Cadiz, an early colony of Tyre, an effigy of Melcarth or Hercules was burned at a yearly festival. Also that at Carthage, greatest of the Tyrian colonies, Dido, who according to the story leapt into a fiery pile, was worshipped as a goddess, for the kings from whom she was descended claimed to personify the god Melcarth. Further, that the god Sandan, also apparently called Hercules by the Greeks, was worshipped at Tarsus and the coins from there show a pyre with the burning god in the midst of it. Frazer also describes a Hittite sculptured rock at Boghaz-Keui, on which there are figures seeming to represent a father-god and a son-god. Frazer guesses that the son-god is Sandan, or Hercules, the son of Zeus:

"Thus it would appear that at Tarsus as at Boghaz-Keui there was a pair of deities, a divine Father and a divine Son, whom the Greeks identified with Zeus and Hercules respectively. If the Baal of Tarsus was a god of fertility, as his attributes clearly imply, his identification with Zeus would be natural, since it was Zeus who, in the belief of the Greeks, sent the fertilizing rain from heaven. And the identification of Sandan with Hercules would be equally natural, since the lion and the death on the pyre were features common to both. Our conclusion then is

[1] Sir James G. Frazer, *Adonis* (The Thinker's Library, No. 30). Watts & Co.

that it was the divine Son, the lion-god, who was burned in effigy or in the person of a human representative at Tarsus, and perhaps at Boghaz-Keui. Semitic parallels suggest that the victim who played the part of the Son of God in the fiery furnace ought in strictness to be the king's son."

This was all very interesting, but how on earth did it affect me? At one period I had taken the interest quite literally and seriously thought of becoming an anthropologist and making a study of primitive religions. But I was learning now not to be quite so simple-minded about interests. I was learning how my mind continually used the ideas of impersonal happenings as a means of thinking, in a dim way, about those of my personal problems which I had not yet been able to admit or think about more directly. So what could this mean, the voluntary self-sacrifice of the God-King? I remembered an earlier discovery,[1] that internal act of the wiping out of myself, of all my plans and purposes and confidence in my own powers, the wiping out of all those strivings after the good things I wanted for myself and others that usually filled my days. But could it be this? Could it possibly be that my pre-occupation with the ritual of the killing of the god was a symbolic way of thinking about this discovery, a discovery which I was always forgetting because it was so utterly opposed to common sense?

I was astonished at the possibilities of this thought. Could it really be that one must voluntarily and deliberately relinquish the idea of good, after having been

[1] *A Life of One's Own.*

taught all one's life that one must strive for it continually? This seemed impossible, and yet I felt close on the trail of something important to me. And what would the result of such an act be? In ancient times it was believed that the fertility of the land depended upon it, and therefore the very existence of the people. I found it easy to be aghast at the waste of good kingly lives for the sake of a fantastic myth. But in fact, was this supreme sacrifice utterly fruitless? Surely it must have been effective in one way, as are all sincerely practised religious ceremonies, it must have relieved the anxieties of the people and kept their hearts up, kept their morale intact, prevented them from giving way to despair in times of trouble.

Was this perhaps the clue for me? I began to experiment. Whenever I felt the clutch of anxiety, particularly in relation to my work, whenever I felt a flood of inferiority lest I should never be able to reach the good I was aiming at, I tried a ritual sacrifice of all my plans and strivings. Instead of straining harder, as I always felt an impulse to do when things were getting difficult, I said: "I am nothing, I know nothing, I want nothing," and with a momentary gesture wiped away all sense of my own existence. The result surprised me so that I could not for the first few times believe it; for not only would all my anxiety fall away, leaving me serene and happy, but also, within a short period, sometimes after only a few minutes, my mind would begin, entirely of itself, throwing up useful ideas on the very problem which I had been struggling with.

Hotfoot after this discovery, I continued to experiment with the gesture. Sometimes I found it was much easier to make than at other times. I discovered also that it was much more effective if there was an emotional abandon in it, if I did not merely state my formula as a cold fact, but felt it in my blood as a giving up of the whole being. And this seemed to involve the idea of giving up myself *to* something. While searching for a way of describing what seemed to happen, a comparison came into my mind—weren't there two brothers in the Bible, one who offered vegetables and God was not pleased, the other a blood sacrifice and God accepted it, Cain and Abel surely? So it occurred to me that the intellectual affirmation of my nothingness was very like a mere vegetable sacrifice—though even that was effective sometimes. Then I remembered also the story of the God of the Old Testament demanding the sacrifice of Abraham's eldest son, but in the end being content simply with his willingness to do it, without the actual killing. Did this story, I wondered, describe a growth in human understanding, was the poet who told the story someone who was able to take life a little less literally than the average man of the time, and able dimly to see that it was not necessary actually to kill a person in order to express the inner truth of deliberate surrender of one's will?

I felt that the implications of this discovery were far-reaching and I hardly knew where to begin in trying to explore them. My first thought was, is it possible that by embracing inner poverty one could escape from the fear of actual poverty, of loss of friends or reputation or livelihood? Echoes of this theme, even from my child-

41

hood, began to crowd in on me. In Kipling's Jungle
Book I had especially loved the story of the Miracle of
Purun Bhagat, a king who set aside his riches and em-
braced poverty, wandering with a begging bowl and—
this was a marvel of marvels to me in those days—all
the animals had come close to him without fear. Just
in the same way the ideas I needed for my work would
now come silently nosing into my mind after I had
given up all attempt to look for them. And then how
I had longed to be rid of all my possessions, especially
trunks with clothes in them, and how I was always trying to plan a single garment which would do for all
occasions, so that I could wander about with no luggage
to bother with, nothing to lose. Nothing to lose, how
that phrase delighted me. Was this perhaps why it was
the lives of the poor that always interested me most
when travelling abroad, why there was always a question in my mind about how they managed to live, these
people who often seemed so happy and yet who had
nothing to look forward to, no spare money to spend on
holidays or on having a good time?

It seemed to me there were two points about this
mental act of momentarily wiping out one's own purposes and desires. First, did it really stop me feeling
anxious and inferior? Second, was the uprush of constructive ideas which I thought followed the act really
a result of it, or was the connection merely accidental?
On the first point I found many observations in my
diary. For instance:

> When I think of all the books I ought to read, instead of
> vowing to read them and then worrying because there

are so many things to do, I can accept the poverty of my knowledge, accept the fact that I don't know all these things, accept the emptiness. And I can do the same when people criticize me, I can accept my poverty in their eyes, say: "Yes, I am like that." And curiously enough, after doing this, I feel actually richer, instead of the lack I had felt before while trying so hard to think up reasons why they were wrong.

The idea that I could perhaps control anxieties and inferiority feelings led me to observe them more closely. Remembering the deep satisfaction I had momentarily found in feeling as if my whole being had been destroyed by an alien force, I had begun to be on the lookout for expressions of the actual desire for pain and failure. Occasionally, in sudden flashes, I became aware that I was often making much more of my troubles than was necessary:

> To-day in the train I could not escape from worry over that lecture I had to give. But suddenly I realized I was whipping myself up to worry, forcing myself to think of it, quite definitely choosing to brood over the discomfort of it. Otherwise why should I think about it all the time? Then I remembered to make my gesture of poverty and immediately all the worry vanished.

Gradually there had come to be no doubt in my mind that there was this force actually driving me on to suffer anxieties and inferiorities, that I had a positive need for them which made me plunge into abject feelings of mental lack whenever I was faced by people who were confident and self-assured and competent. And again and again I found I could avoid it by forestalling it.

AN EXPERIMENT IN LEISURE

Granted then that this thing existed, this desire for the depths of self-abasement and that in some measure I had learnt how to deal with it, was I any nearer understanding its meaning? At first sight it was obviously a perverse thing, a morbid desire for failure that could only lead to disaster. But what if one saw it in a wider context? What if this instinct for self-abasement was perhaps a primitive undeveloped form of something else? What if the self-inflicted inferiorities and pains and self-destroyings were merely the result of failure to understand the real meaning of an impulse whose proper expression was something quite different? Did this perhaps explain the conflict of expert opinion as to whether the desire to suffer were perverse or normal? In occasional flashes I guessed what might be the final outcome of the impulse, but I could not reason it out, nor did I find that deliberate reading of books on psychology made the matter any clearer, it only confused me. I could, therefore, only state the problem to myself and wait for clues.

Gradually I found that I was getting some help from books, but not from scientific ones. It was images from myths, poetry, fairy tales that seemed most relevant to my problem.

Here is a section from my diary at the time:

. . . Several times when I've tried this wiping out of my sense of self, and all the anxieties of things I ought to do and be have fallen away, I have felt it like the dropping of a burden—then I suddenly remembered Christian's burden. Is this what Bunyan meant? Is the sense of self and of individual responsibility and of sin all part of the

44

same thing? When Adam and Eve ate of the tree of knowledge, did that mean becoming self-conscious? They also became aware of shame, of inferiority; with becoming aware of self, they also became aware of "not self" (which the story calls God), and were overwhelmed by the thought. So was Christian. He thought he would be overwhelmed by it in fire and brimstone. And he tried legal morality to ease his conscience and appease this terrifying thing—but he was only the more terrified that the rock of it would fall and crush him—Wasn't it the same with the rich young man in the Bible? He said he had kept the moral rules all his life but was still anxious about salvation. And he was told to embrace poverty, literally.

And then Odysseus, suffering was imposed on him as a punishment because he had killed the son of Poseidon, God of the Sea. If gods are psychic forces, what was Poseidon and why am I so haunted by the description of how Odysseus and his men arrived at the cave of Polyphemos?

"Now when we had come to the land that lies hard by, we saw a cave on the border near to the sea, lofty and roofed over with laurels, and there many flocks of sheep and goats were used to rest. And about it a high outer court was built with stones, deep bedded, and with tall pines and oaks with their high crown of leaves. And a man was wont to sleep therein, of monstrous size, who shepherded his flocks alone and afar, and was not conversant with others, but dwelt apart in lawlessness of mind. Yea, for he was a monstrous thing and fashioned marvellously, nor was he like to any man that lives by bread, but like a wooded peak of the towering hills, which stands out apart and alone from others." [1]

[1] *The Odyssey of Homer*, Butcher and Lang, pp. 139–40.

AN EXPERIMENT IN LEISURE

As God of the Sea, wouldn't Poseidon perhaps be God of all that is "without form and void", the unknown factor both in oneself and as mirrored in the outer world? And his son, the Titan, perhaps, something that emerges from the unknown part of oneself? . . .

Wasn't it Menelaus who forgot to sacrifice to the gods and so was becalmed and couldn't get on with his journey? Those ritual sacrifices, I used to think how barbarous they were, what a waste of time and animals—but I'm not so sure, obviously there was a useful effect, not on hypothetical gods, but on the living men. In all the myths, if you offend the gods by ignoring them, they take revenge. But it is not only the "good" gods. You must placate not only your conscience, not only Zeus and Athene who demand that you act justly and wisely, but also the "bad" ones, the giants and Titans; if you offend them perhaps not even Zeus will be able to help you—but only the psycho-analyst. This one-eyed giant, Polyphemos, who lived on milk in a dirty cave—surely a very primitive and infantile stage—and Odysseus in his pride of will and cunning reason thought he could ride roughshod over him—thought, I suppose, that he could do as he liked with the half-blind, Titanic forces within himself. I've met people who have done that, and who've had years of expiation afterwards, just as Odysseus had. I must have done it myself time and again—thought in the arrogance of my will that I would do what seemed reasonable and ignore the titanic force of desire. I suppose I have even blinded it as Odysseus did, driven it down into darkness for fear it would otherwise destroy me. Yes, surely it's what I've done with this desire to suffer, nearly wrecking myself dozens of times, as Odysseus did too, because I had not recognized it as one of the sons of the gods. . . . To accept the unknown factors in oneself, this is obviously a terrific task. It's easier to make oneself into a magic lan-

46

tern and project them on to the screen of an outer world of gods and giants. This unknown factor, "x", the "not-self", it's always there, even if you have so blown up your ego that you feel yourself dictator of the world, there are still the stars that are "not you". However much you know there is always the immeasurable gulf of what you don't know. And it's no good trying to push away the idea of it. So why not sacrifice to the "x" (what a chilly name for the gods!) instead of trying to build frantic bulwarks against it, why not ritualize my knowledge of my own smallness and make it a bearable thought?

. . . Christian and Odysseus were opposite types of character; obviously in Christian the overwhelming power of the "not-self" filled him with a continual sense of guilt, of expectation of destruction. But Odysseus was continually aware of his own power and the love of exercising it. He says of himself:

"Such an one was I in war, but the labour of the field I never loved, nor home-keeping thrift, that breeds brave children, but galleys with their oars were dear to me, and wars and polished shafts and darts—baneful things whereat others used to shudder. But that, methinks, was dear to me which god put in my heart, for divers men take delight in divers deeds."

So I think he hardly gave a thought to the terrors of the unknown factor, and he had to make an expedition to the underworld before he could be brought to realize how he must expiate his offence.

I thought: 'Obviously my problems are more like those of Christian than of Odysseus.' And yet there was so much in *Pilgrim's Progress* that did not mean

47

anything to me at all, so much in the Odyssey that roused deep echoes of importance. Perhaps Odysseus was the eternal opposite of everything that I thought I was, perhaps he stood for the type of those people who, I had found by experience, looked on all my struggles as pointless, morbid, a lot of fuss about nothing. And yet there was someone in the Odyssey with whom I could claim kinship. For Telemachus says:

"As for me I am nowise strong like him to ward mine own; verily to the end of my days shall I be a weakling and all unskilled in prowess. Truly I would defend me if but strength were mine; for deeds past sufferance have now been wrought, and now my house is wasted utterly beyond pretence of right."

I wondered, if you were born the sort of person who is more aware of the other person's strength than of your own, what are you to do about it? Christian's pilgrimage gave me little hint at first, so much of the symbolism was alien; and Telemachus did not solve his own problem at all, he merely searched for and finally relied upon the strength of his father, as women do when they fall in love with such a man as Odysseus was. But was there no Odyssey of those who were continually aware of their own weakness?

One thing puzzled me especially: belief in magic, so the experts say, is rooted in a childish misunderstanding of the laws of cause and effect. One reads that the belief of barbarous people that they can definitely influence the natural laws of weather and changing seasons

CHAPTER FOUR

and all that makes for fertility of the land, by this sort of magic play-acting, is the result of a childish confusion between fact and fancy. I had read many books on the child's ways of thinking, on savage ways of thinking, on the "unconscious" mind's ways of thinking, and from all these I had gained an impression of the mind's infinite capacity for deceiving itself. I had gathered that myths and fairy tales and magic rituals were all roundabout ways of pretending you could get what you wanted without the trouble of common-sense working for it, hence they were no concern of the truly adult person except to smile at and discard. But here was I, trying as well as I knew how, to reach an adult standard of independence in thought and action, yet finding that the more I tried the more images from these apparently infantile ways of thinking flooded into my mind. And also I was finding that they did not come in shamefacedly, as with a sense of something I should have outgrown, but with a sense of power that beckoned me onward. Could this sense really be an illusion, a siren voice drawing me on to disaster? The still glow that surrounded some of these images in my mind, images of the burning god, of Adonis and Odysseus, did it come because they satisfied surreptitiously some crude infantile desire that I ought to have left behind long ago? I could not believe that it was so, for I had had enough psycho-analytic experience to recognize the feeling of disreputable infantile desires, there was a narrow furtiveness about them that was utterly different from the broad stillness of these other images. Also I had learnt how to observe in myself numberless examples of the

49

AN EXPERIMENT IN LEISURE

mind deceiving itself, when I found myself indulging in what I had called "blind thinking". But the kind of thinking that brought these other images was of a quite different quality, it had a feeling of greatest stillness and austerity; instead of grabbing after pleasures like a burrowing mole as blind reverie did, it hung suspended and watchful like a hovering kestrel. So far I had found nothing in the books to suggest that such a way of thinking even existed, for if it was not idle daydreaming, it certainly was not like any process of reasoning that I had ever heard described.

Then one day I was shown a book [1] which gave me a clue. For here I found it stated that the imagination uses mental images in two ways: it uses them as "wishfulfilments", as a means of evading hard facts; but it also uses them as a way of thinking about hard facts, as an instrument, not for the evading of truth, but for reaching it. And, such is the curious expandibility of symbols, both these uses can be combined in a single image. So it was quite possible that the image of killing the human representative of a god could directly satisfy primitive desires to inflict pain, or to suffer pain, or to destroy an authority that thwarted one's desires; but at the same time it could dimly foreshadow the truth of a purely psychic process for which no more direct language was available. So although my interest in the killing of the god could and probably did spring partly from the fact that I had many infantile desires that I had not been able to admit, this need not make the imagery useless from the point of view of

[1] Silberer, *Problems of Mysticism and its Symbolism.*

50

CHAPTER FOUR

adult problems of discovery, for I read also that to understand any living process properly you must take into account, not only where it has come from, but also where it is going to.

CHAPTER FIVE

THIS attempt to follow the clues of feeling had led me to become aware of an impulse, which, when not recognized, had driven me into useless misery; but when recognized and deliberately allowed, it seemed to have an opposite effect. In fact, I thought that if I could always deliberately allow it, my life would be very different, infinitely richer and without fear. But apparently I could only rarely allow it, most of the day I was forbidding this impulse, building up bulwarks to try and protect my identity. Why? I thought the answer to this might be partly connected with the question of what it was I had to submit to. I knew well enough by now that when part of one's mind behaved rebelliously it was often because there was some hidden misunderstanding, a preconceived idea, often utterly fantastic, which could not be corrected because it had never been put into words. But I knew also that if I kept strict enough watch on the wanderings of my mind it would sooner or later lead me to the idea that was causing the trouble ; so I continued with my method, but looked especially for ideas of what it might be, against which I so urgently needed protection.

My first thoughts were of the peculiar inner contentment that followed whenever I found it possible to achieve real muscular relaxation. There was a note in my diary:

> I can sink down, out of my head, into a deeper part of my body, usually somewhere in my spine between my shoulder blades, where there are no thoughts, or at least thoughts are only incidental—it produces a most serene sort of happiness, and it is somehow very profane—not that I like it any the less for that.

This feeling had a quality of goodness about it, like the "goodness" of a cat lying in the sun. But also it seemed to involve facing something that was "other". I found I had written:

> ... direct contact, facing "something", which is I think inside me, without words or purposes or protection, a direct touching of something which feels like the raw experience of being alive—coming face to face with something inside you, something intensely living—but it's certainly not "thinking about" something inside you ...

I had not known how to explain it, but had simply called it "the inner fact". It had a warmth and certainty about it, and in my notes I found:

> ... this inner fact has sometimes a curious quality of space, an inner spaceless space where all is accomplished ... and sometimes when enjoying looking across a wide view of country, I feel there is as much size of universe opening through and behind me as there is out in front— a sort of through-the-looking-glassland.

Whenever I found it possible to submit myself to this inner fact I found quick recuperation of both mind and body, but I could only very rarely do it. It seemed that though my experience continued to tell me that the inner fact of being alive was definitely good, there was still a part of my mind that did not believe this at all; so I continued to keep watch on my thoughts in order to find out what this other part of my mind did believe.

There was one place where I saw more things that gave me the warm intimate feeling of importance than almost anywhere else and that was the Zoo. I tried to describe some of these to find why they were important.

'... the wrinkled forehead of that little she-bear, climbing the iron-plated tree in her cage and biting the wood at the top—those wrinkles on her forehead, like a desperate struggle to understand, something striving to break through, express itself—she came to the bars and put a hand through to take a bit of bread, but it was almost a dead hand, no, not that, simply unused, the five long claws all stuck together like a mummied hand —for all those five claws she could only manage to hold the bread at all by a clumsy shuffling of the palms ... beyond in the den, that huge shaggy brown bear, lying on his side, utterly lazy, vaguely scratching his chest with one huge paw, and completely abandoned to the first spring sun.

'... that rhinoceros, a comic titan, like a huge frowsty old woman with knickers slipping down—but restless now, charging across the yard, only just wheeling in time to avoid crashing into the bars—exasperated —now he's trying a bath, but that won't do either— what a speed there is in his lumbering run, body like a torpedo—and blind, chaotic, bound-down power.

CHAPTER FIVE

'. . . a lion and lioness, in an outside cage, so close behind me while I was watching the wading birds, it shocked me to find them there—like finding someone you know waiting silently behind you. Now the lion has got up and leapt to that wooden platform in the corner, he's sharpening his claws—I can see his curious lean loins, so small and lithe after that great head—now he's lying down, laying his head sideways on his paws, a childlike weariness and unconcern. There's the lioness, in front, better proportioned, staring, staring, she won't attend to me, though she looks a little embarrassed. Now she's getting up, having a good stretch, front paws first, now she's leapt on to his ledge and nuzzled his face—but there isn't really room for her. He's opened his eyes, stretching wide his mouth into a little yawning howl of petulant boredom—"Oh, DON'T bother me"—so she comes down again to go on staring. Do they know they are bored, not using themselves or spending themselves, a blind boredom?

'. . . that dromedary, dumbness of flesh, so queerly comic.

'. . . there's a cormorant lustily flapping his wings, as intense and absorbed with himself as that little girl over there who is so solemnly stamping her feet.

' In the humming-bird house, chirps and scraps of half-finished songs from the other side where the bigger birds are, I can feel the height of dark trees above me and the damp stillness of forests. Then these humming birds, a little bedraggled most of them, yet they make me full of wanting to laugh, like the lazy bear did, there's no struggle to express here, or boredom, they are

55

so full of being themselves, such an nth degree of concentrated living, it seems to spread round them, vibrat-
ing the air in a purple sheen, a sort of ultra-violet ray
that stabs my eyes—it even blurs the outline of their
tiny heads. What a speeding up of the tempo and tem-
perature of living—and I've just been looking at the
tortoises.'

Then I remembered some of the things that had
delighted me so in my son when he was just beginning
to grow out of babyhood.

'. . . J's sudden determination that he must have one
thing and one thing only, yesterday his all-of-a-sudden
feeling that he must have that dirty old bit of sponge to
take to bed with him . . . and the way, out in the road,
he will go scudding off after anything that catches his
fancy, that girl with a yellow coat who was laughing,
then a little girl, and then a black dog.

'. . . the enthusiasm with which he suddenly decides
he wants his pot and trots along the passage, and the
chirrups of satisfaction when he's finished.

'. . . the way he looks up with that little confiding
smile of enjoyment, as he did when he climbed up on to
the seat beside me in the Park.'

Looking over these interests, it seemed that my mind
was now continually preoccupied with a vague sense of
the power of feeling and desire in living things; that is,
at least, whenever I managed to slip beyond my daily
purposes enough to know what I really was interested
in. For it was only when achieving what I had called
" wide-perceiving" that those stirrings of warmth
emerged which seemed to be such important clues to

what I really wanted. I had a particular example of this one day when, sitting bored at a meeting, I found myself watching someone in the crowd who filled me with jealous and depressed admiration.

'. . . Rather fun to look like that, fringe so jaunty, could I grow one? Where did she get that jumper, very up-to-date, how could I look more like that, she's so sure of herself, I wish I could be . . .'

Then, exasperated with boredom and envy I had remembered to wipe out my own hankerings deliberately, and had at once been as delighted as I had by the rhinoceros or the humming bird:

'I feel the power of her, the curious profile, uncouth a little, restlessness, must be doing something, latent possibility of blazing anger.'

Whenever I could remember to forget my purposes I began to catch the same feeling:

'In the tube was a workman, middle-aged, in brown overalls but a clean stiff collar, specs on the end of his nose, big hands, thin, lanky; long helpless feet. Why so real? So lovable? Maybe very tiresome at home, full of fads, but a person, not lovable because you want his successes parasitically for yourself, but because he's so much himself.'

Then I came across a note written several years before:

'. . . last night I felt myself into my heart, out of my head, and then became aware of this sense of self, much bigger, unlimited, like the self in music which I cannot believe to be myself but shut away and try to understand from outside. But now I found myself being afraid of the bigness of this self which I yet knew was me because I felt its movements. I kept wanting to scuttle back into my head, feeling like the old woman in the folk-song: "This is none of I".'

And this reminded me how there were times, in listening to certain kinds of music, when I suddenly slipped from the feeling that the composer was telling me something to the feeling that the music was something that was happening to me. But what so often kept me from this second way of listening, which was much the most satisfying, was the feeling that the music was the experience of gods or whole races of men, it was so big it could have nothing to do with me and my trivial life—except as something to watch and delight in afar off.

At about this time I also found another line of interest that seemed to be converging in the same direction. In the books that I had to read in connection with my work, I met continual reference to the idea that:

> "The conduct through life of what we call our ego is essentially passive . . . we are 'lived' by unknown and uncontrollable forces." [1]

I read that the name of "ID" or "IT" had been given to "whatever in our nature is impersonal and, so to speak, subject to natural law"; also that this ID was very powerful but apparently liable to extraordinary blindness and stupidity.

For I read:

> ". . . it is the unknown ID, and not the conscious intelligence which is responsible for disease. . . . Do you

[1] Quotation from Freud's preface to Groddeck's *The Book of the IT*.

58

find it impossible that a being that has produced from spermatozoon and egg a man's brain and a man's heart can also bring forth cancer or pneumonia, or a dropping of the womb?" [1]

Although I told myself that it was only a hypothesis, I was continually preoccupied with this idea. I thought of the mysterious retentiveness of habit in this force, which could build up from the single cell the characteristics of its ancestors; I thought also of the wreckage that it could cause when misunderstood, when dammed up and forced to break through the dykes of normal living. I began to feel its power everywhere.

' Once you become aware of the force of unconscious processes there's no going back and pretending you don't see it.

'. . . the intensity of B. (aged eight) who will scream for hours, till she is utterly exhausted, because she knows no other way to get what she needs; of the dung beetle at Le Levandou pushing his ball again and again up the sand, however often it fell back because it was too big; of that child perpetually stealing, however often she was punished, till she was told what she needed to know.'

But if this force was a fact, and I had no doubt that it was, how did it connect with my inner fact; this tempestuous blindness which I observed in other people and animals, what had it to do with that inner overpowering serenity which I experienced during moments of relaxation?

In adolescence I had worshipped Nature as God.

[1] Groddeck, op. cit., p. 20.

AN EXPERIMENT IN LEISURE

But now I happened to read, with a shock of how well it fitted my thought at the moment:

"It seems to me that painters as a rule represent the Saviour, both on the cross and taken down from it, with great beauty still upon His face. But . . . this (picture) was the presentment of a poor mangled body which had evidently suffered unbearable anguish even before its crucifixion, full of wounds and bruises, marks of the violence of soldiers and people, and of the bitterness of the moment when He had fallen with the cross—all this combined with the anguish of the actual crucifixion . . .

"The thought steps in, whether one likes it or no, that death is so terrible and so powerful, that even He who conquered it in His miracles during life was unable to triumph over it at the last. . . . Nature appears to one, looking at this picture, as some huge, implacable, dumb monster; or still better—a stranger simile—some enormous mechanical engine of modern days which has seized and crushed and swallowed up a great and invaluable Being, a Being worth nature and all her laws, worth the whole earth, which was perhaps created merely for the sake of the advent of that Being." [1]

I thought again of Freud's saying: 'We are "lived" by unknown and uncontrollable forces.' I had once felt a dim terror at the thought that I myself might not exist at all as a person, but only as a focusing point for these terrific forces. Then one night, after thinking over these things, I had a before-sleep image which unfolded itself before my eyes like a coloured moving-picture:

'. . . a serpent, it was more than a snake, . p).)aching

[1] *The Idiot*, Fyodor Dostoyevsky, New American Library.

me, slowly drifting, but inevitably towards me, on the surface of a hot glowing ooze, so that the coils of its great body and the swirls of the ooze were not separate, but writhing together. I felt a kind of remote horror, that I must hold tight on myself and wait for it to pass, not really doubting my power to resist, but knowing I must.'

Then I wrote:

'. . . Is this my love? The "Nature" that killed Jesus? Is this my love? This blind, steaming serpent of life emerging from the ooze, is this my love? Is this what I must submit to?'

Some weeks after this image came another:

'Tuesday. With a great struggle I wrote for two hours this afternoon. Then gave up with a headache and a recurring feeling that what I was struggling to do was tempting forces I had no notion of, arousing anger of gods or devils. When in bed I turned inwards to find my spacious inner fact, but in place of the usual feeling of delight I saw the image of a huge stinging centipede. I tried not to shrink from it but to accept it, there, at the heart of what I felt to be most intimately me. But more sinister images followed, indescribable. I thought: "I suppose if I did not know that these are merely images that will pass, that would be madness." I remembered those temptations of the mediæval mystics which I had seen pictures of. Is this what happens? Once you begin to explore to find the face of your love you also find the face of your hates and fears—the face of the devil. Instinctively I clutched out for help to a name most associated in my mind with power over demons—

and at the word "Jesus" all the images disappeared, leaving me sane and comfortable.'

Having learnt that fears must be faced, not ignored, I decided that the time had come for me to go in deliberate search of the Devil, to find out what my idea of evil was.

By following up the interest in witchcraft I had already guessed at the importance of this theme and at the time thought I had sufficiently understood it. But evidently I had not understood enough, or rather, as I was slowly finding out, everything that one thinks one understands has to be understood over and over again, in its different aspects, each time with the same new shock of discovery.   So I had to ask now, what was the meaning of this poisonous insect?   It was a long time before I could even begin to answer this question, but several weeks after the appearance of the centipede, I tried one day deliberately sinking back into myself to see if it was still there.   It was, but as I watched I felt it slowly dissolving as if in some strong digestive juice.

After this image my first thought was that perhaps even cruel and poisoning and destroying forces can be used for one's own needs, if only one does not fight, that perhaps even they are necessary for one's needs, a necessary part of mental creation, just as acceptance of violent power is a necessary part of physical creation.   I thought: 'Is this perhaps the answer to my doubts about nature, nature pictured as a destroying insect?   (In *The Idiot* wasn't there also a dream of a loathsome insect that bit the dog's tongue?)   Is it perhaps that raw nature is, or can be, evil, but that nature can be digested by turning the full wide ray of awareness upon it?' But though I could guess this possibility in general, I had to go a long way round before I could be sure of its implications. Sometimes I became very depressed about my search:

'Why did I think I could look for the Devil? It seems a bit arrogant; do I think I could face him when I met him? But I must be clear where evil is. Is it cruelty? Not cruelty by itself, for animals are cruel to each other, it's cruel when the ichneumon fly grub eats away the caterpillar's inside, or an owl kills a mouse— but it is not evil. But when men torture each other, delighting in each other's pain, surely this is evil? Are they responsible for what they do? Jesus said that the people who tortured Him were not.

'Last week I gave up looking for the Devil, I decided I couldn't face it. I had a dream, in which I seemed all night to be struggling with something that forced me downwards. It seemed evil but it occurs to me now that it was not evil, for the last few days I have found many of the things I love much more in physical life.'

But although I could interpret the dream to my own satisfaction, there was all the difference in the world between recognizing intellectually that there could be good in being forced downwards, and in letting oneself go to the depths. In moments of clear seeing when alone and recollected I could know that my inner fact was good and that the centipede could be digested, but as soon as I had to take part in ordinary affairs then I certainly behaved as though there were some unknown danger to guard against. What this was I could not tell but my thoughts continued to hover round the idea of the ID:

'. . . this queer power which can build up from the single cell the characteristics of its ancestors . . . "the body is a big sagacity" . . . the idea of something trying to express itself . . . and out of it all comes an idea that strikes with a shock of difference against what I'd thought of God, something much too near . . . "God, that is not your name", not God as conscience, parent, authority, but God as experience . . . I have been trying to find some symbol for this, something less vague—I don't seem able to use Christian symbols . . . somehow at the moment it seems to need a much more primitive barbaric symbolism, there's a gleam of brazen metal at the back of my thought.'

This glimpse of another theme cropping up puzzled me. What on earth could a gleam of brazen metal have to do with my problem? I found that I could not answer this question by any direct approach. But I remembered a method that I had been told of by a man who had especially studied the habits of this thing called the ID. He had said that if an adult could bring himself to write a fairy tale, simply letting the story flow and describing whatever impossible happenings occurred to him, without any forethought or criticism, then the story would show in allegorical terms just what was going on in the deeper levels of his mind. And I remembered that I had tried to do this and had managed to write a story, but had been quite unable to finish it.

CHAPTER FIVE

After writing it I could not see at all what it was all about, but I now thought I would look at it again, being reminded of it by this intruding brazen gleam which was puzzling me.

CHAPTER SIX

I

'A LITTLE boy sat by an attic window and looked down on the busyness of Covent Garden. The attic was empty and dirty and he was hungry. He didn't know where his parents were. Perhaps they had gone away and left him—and he had no idea what he was going to do. Presently he got up and wandered downstairs out into the warm sunlight and thick smell of apples. The smell so enticed him, he flicked one off a corner of a barrow as he sauntered by, and slipped it in his pocket. Nobody saw him, and when well into the next street he took it out and began to bite hungrily. The apple was good, crisp to his teeth, but before he had got half through he began to feel curious sensations all over him. . . . He felt himself swelling and swelling and his sense of who he was getting dimmer and dimmer, till at last he felt himself slipping away altogether. But people who were walking in Drury Lane saw a large green melon rolling in the gutter. Nobody took much notice of it amongst all the shuffle and bustle, but finally it got kicked down the hill and started off rolling and bumping towards the Embankment. It gained such speed that when it hit the stone wall at the edge of the water it burst, splashing its red flesh against the grey stone, and throwing its pips so high that the wind caught them and they were blown over into the river. A little old woman leaning against the parapet, saw them fall and idly watched them sink. When they were almost out of sight she thought she saw them begin to wriggle, as if they had turned into little fishes. And actually they had. They were a shoal of little fishes and they darted away into the deep parts of the river.

'The little fishes swam down the river till the water became salter and salter and cleaner and cleaner and at last they were out in the open sea. And here they swam about for days, exploring. Sometimes they dived down as far as they could go, and found shells and bits of wrecked ships covered all over with waving sea-weed; and sometimes they rose to the top, past big fishes and little fishes up to the sunlight and white-horse waves. After a bit they had found out the sort of place the sea was and they wanted someone to play with; but all the creatures they had met so far seemed too busy, or else so big that they were frightening to little fishes and looked as if they would eat them, or else so timid like hermit crabs, that they drew their heads inside their shells as soon as the play began. So the little fishes went farther afield to look for someone to play with, always following their noses. Following their noses they left the North Sea and went away down the English Channel into the great Atlantic. Here they stayed for many days, gradually drifting south where the sea was warm, and then, still following their noses, they one day rounded Cape Horn and swam into the Pacific. But still they found no one to play with them, and they went on and on into the deep waters of the ocean. Then one day when they were so deep down that no light from the sun ever brought even a glimmer out of the blackness, and all the fishes had to carry their own green phosphorus lights, they came upon something to play with—it shone out in the light from the fishes' lamps, gleaming white whenever one of them swam near it, gleams of white against the inky mud: the skeleton of a man.

'At first the little fishes were quite content playing hide-and-seek among the arches of its ribs, and in and out of the dark sockets of its eyes, but after a while they grew tired of this and the everlasting green light from the phosphorescent lamps and they said, "Let's find something bright to dress it in." So they set off again, back from the deepest pit of the Pacific Ocean, back towards Cape Horn. But this time they did not go round the Cape, but took a short cut through the channel that divides the land of the Patagonians on the one side and the Island of Flaming Fires on the other. And when they had come through this, they wandered up the coast of Brazil, always following their noses. Then one day they began to find that the clear clean sea was suddenly muddied and cloudy, and they thought of the day long ago when they had swum out of the mouth of the Thames; but they were now far out from the land and they did not understand it at all. So they swam up to the surface and poked their heads out to see what might be happening. There were no ships and there was no land, but all about them were little jumping flecks of gold and crimson and green.

CHAPTER SIX

At first they were too delighted to do anything but stare. Then the eldest of the fishes made a leap at the nearest dancing fleck and caught something in his mouth. It was a green parrot's feather. For the little fishes had come, without knowing it, just to the place where the waters of the Amazon sweep far out into the sea, and bring with them all the feathers that have dropped from gay coloured birds of the forest and the swamp, from parrots and flamingoes. And now that the other little fishes had seen what it was, they each caught a feather of the colour they liked best, and then, without waiting a moment, they all turned and set off again for the Black Pit of the Pacific Ocean.

'After many weeks of swimming they were back again above the spot where their plaything lay; and then they began to drop down and down, through water five miles deep, getting darker and darker all the time, but they were very pleased with themselves because they thought of the bright colours they were bringing. At last they reached the inky black mud, so black that they could not see it, they only knew it was there by a soft sticky feeling. But surely it had not been as dark as this before, where were the queer-looking deep-sea fishes with their green lights? Their hearts sank as they wondered how they would ever find their plaything again in the pitch darkness. Then in the distance they caught sight of the faintest green glimmer, and darting up to it they found a great bony fish, shaped like a triangle with a long spike for a nose and the green lamp hanging at the end of it. They crowded round him and asked anxiously where all the others had gone.

He told them rather crossly that of course there were no light-fishes about, it was not the season for them, they all went off this time of year to the Doldrums to have their lights cleaned and refilled—and he himself would be off in a minute, he had only got left behind because he was having a nap and had not noticed the time. Then with a sudden flick of his triangular body, he darted into the blackness and was gone, knocking the little fishes out of his way. It was so sudden, they were left gasping, and the coloured feathers that they had carried in their mouths all the way from the Amazon floated away before they could realize what was happening.

'At first the little fishes were quite speechless with disappointment, then it occurred to them that the feathers wouldn't be much good without any light to see them by, and anyway, how were they ever going to find their plaything again? Then the eldest of the fishes said suddenly: "But of course, we must follow our noses!" and straight away they darted off, and in a minute found themselves nosing in and out of the arches of their plaything, the arches that they knew were white and shining although they could not see them.

' But soon they got tired of playing in the pitch darkness, so they all collected inside the skull and had a committee meeting about what was to be done. Some thought they had better go off and try to find the Doldrums and see if they couldn't perhaps get hold of lights too. But the eldest said: "Those green lights aren't much catch even when you have got them. Let's go up to the top and see if the sun couldn't help us." This seemed a good idea so they set off at once, swimming up and up and up through five miles height of water, and at last saw pale flickerings of sunlight above them, so that with one flick of their tails they shot out into the air. The daylight was so lovely after depths of gloom that for several days they just splashed about enjoying themselves, seeing how high they could jump, and then lying quite still rocking on the waves. But after a bit they began to wonder how the sun would be able to help them. Every morning they met together just as the sun appeared over the edge of the sea, and shouted their difficulty in chorus—but day after day they got no answer, the sun just smiled down on them, but he never said anything. And day after day they basked and played, till at the end of a month they began to feel homesick for their plaything. Then one day the eldest fish happened to take a look at the others and said: "Goodness, what a funny colour you are!" And the other fishes said: "Funny colour yourself!" And so they were, they had all of them basked so long in the sun that their scales had turned to a beautiful golden bronze. And the eldest fish said: "Praps this is the Sun's answer, praps this will do instead of lamps. Let's go and see." So they all dived back into the depths, swimming down and down and down. When they had done about the first mile they met a sword fish. "Where are you going?" he said. "To the bottom of the Pacific's Blackest Pit," they said. "Oh, but you can't go there," said the sword-fish. "You'll be crushed to death by the five miles weight of water; the fishes that live there all have special bones

and if ever they come up to the top, they burst."
"But we've been," said the little fishes, and went on
their way. And after three days they knew by the
tickling in their noses that they were nearly back again.
But this time it was not quite so inky black. Wherever
they went there was a very faint golden glow, shining
out from the bronze of their scales. And when they
reached the inky black mud they could just see each
other against the inkiness, and when they came to their
plaything they could just see it faintly glimmering, and
the black hollows of its eyes. But by now they were not
content with dim hide-and-seek, they wanted to take
their plaything back with them into the waves and the
sun. So they had another committee to decide how to
lift it up to the top of the sea.

'After a good deal of argument they all set to work
to spin. Of course they had no spinning wheels, but
they span inside themselves like a spider does, and when
they swam round and round their plaything, little
bronze coloured silk threads came out of their mouths
and were woven in and out, till they had made an
immense bronze coloured cocoon of softest silk.
"Now," they said proudly, "the bones will not fall
apart or be damaged when we lift it." Then when
all was finished, they wriggled their noses into the mud
beneath it and tried to raise it upwards. But though
they struggled with all their might they could not move
it a single inch.

'After a great deal of pushing and tugging, they gave
it up, and had a rest while they wondered what to do
next. Suddenly the youngest fish said: "Supposing the

72

bottom of the sea came to the top!"—and the others all snorted. "But it might, you know," went on the youngest, "there might be an eruption." The others snorted all the more, especially those who did not know what an eruption meant. But the eldest fish said, "Let us follow our noses and perhaps we will come upon someone who will help us." So off they set once more and they swam right round the world. But they did not find anyone to help them, in fact no one would even stop long enough to hear what it was they wanted.

'Then one day when they were in the cold seas of the north, they saw a man looking over the side of a boat and they decided to ask him; for up till now they had not thought of asking a human being what to do. But this man did not seem as busy as everyone else had been, and he looked down into the water at them, and then pointed towards the land: "Over there is the mouth of a river and if you swim up it for three days you will then find someone who can tell everyone all the things he wants to know." So the fishes thanked him, but they were no longer little fishes, for during all their travels they had grown big and strong and each of them now was a twenty-pound salmon. And off they went to the mouth of the river and they swam up it for three days.

'On the evening of the third day they came to a place where the river narrowed between dark rocks and came crashing down over a fall. This was nothing to the salmon however, they leapt up it without a thought, but only to find themselves hopelessly entangled in nets.

73

They lashed about looking for a way out, and then when it was quite dark they heard the voices of men and saw a light coming near. "This is what comes of asking other people's advice and not following our noses," said the eldest salmon. And it was his last remark, for at that moment he was pierced with a gaff and hauled on to the bank.

'And that was the last of the shoal of little fishes, for soon they were all cut up and neatly packed away in round tins, all ready to be eaten with salad for Sunday supper.'

2

'In Peckham Rye there was a little old woman who never would eat anything out of tins, she said: "You never know and it's better to take no risks!" But one evening she went to Sunday supper with some friends and they quite forgot that she would never eat anything out of tins till the supper was all put ready on the table. Then they thought: "But we need not tell her!" . . . and when she came in they mentioned casually that a friend of theirs had been up north and sent them a fine salmon he'd caught. So the little old woman ate her supper quite happily and afterwards went home to the room where she lived by herself.

'Her friends did not meet her again for several days, and when they did they were a little puzzled about her, for she began asking such curious questions. She wanted to know all about boats that went exploring to the North Pole. This went on for some weeks, she was suddenly taking an interest in all sorts of out-of-the-way things. And her friends said : "She has never been the same since that night she ate the tinned salmon."

'The little old woman herself did not know what had happened. For she had woken up the morning after the supper with her friends, saying over and over to herself: "The bottom of the sea must come to the top, the bottom of the sea must come to the top." Then some phrase she might have heard years ago at school kept coming into her head, as if a teacher was always asking her something she could not answer: "What is the Magnetic North? Where is the Magnetic North? What—what—where—Magnetic?" It was so exasperating. After a bit, in order to do something and perhaps get it out of her mind, she went off to the Public Library and looked up all the papers to see if there was anything about explorations to the North Pole. Sure enough there was an account of an expedition just about to set off, it described the boat, the date and the place of sailing. "Now," she thought, "praps some of these people could ease my mind about this bothersome Magnetic North business." And that night she dreamt that she had somehow got on to the boat for the North Pole, and was leaning over the side watching the water when a fish poked its head up at her and said: "You must make a gong of seven metals and let its sound ring in the stillness of the Magnetic Pole." When she woke up in the morning, she said: "Oh, bother all this," and tried to forget it; but do what she would, she could not help saying over and over again: "You must make a gong of seven metals." Instead of fading as the day went on, as most dreams do, the

75

phrase became more and more insistent, so that when she went out to buy a herring for her lunch, she intended to say: "Will you cut the head off and bone it for me?" but actually found herself saying: "You must make a gong of seven metals." This terrified her, she felt she was going mad, and she rushed off without waiting for her herring. After a long time of fierce walking (she was a little lame, but made up in energy what she lacked in ease) she came to an open square and sat down on a seat, exhausted. If she could not run away from her thought, why not run into it? Seven metals, what might those be? Iron was one— and then there'd be gold and silver, and tin as well, and copper and lead. But that was only six. There must be a seventh, she'd think of it soon. Suddenly she found she'd been sitting there an hour, brooding over the fish's formula. How insistent her thoughts were, she was getting quite scared at their power. She tried to force her mind to think of all the things she ought to be doing at home, but it was no good, only the formula rang round and round in her head. In desperation she got up, saying to herself: "It's better to do mad things than to be mad. I'll go and find those metals, then praps I'll get it off my mind." She chose the first street turning out of the square, not knowing at all where it went, indeed she did not know where she was at all, she had wandered into a part of the city that was strange to her. But soon she came to an empty place where some houses had been pulled down and there was a lot of rubbish about. Just ahead, lying in the dust, was a horse-shoe. "One," she said,

and snatched it up. Close to it was an old tin can and
a dirty sack. "Two," she said, as she picked up the
can and put it into the sack with the horse-shoe. Then
she stopped to think a minute, took out her purse and
looked in. There was a penny and a sixpence, that
was all. "Three, four!" she said triumphantly. But
her face fell again. "It won't be very big," she thought,
so she stooped down and began filling up her sack with
some more tin cans. Lying beside one of them she saw
a bit of wood that had once been painted green.
Absent-mindedly she turned it over and saw that it was
a broken thermometer. It was only the stem that was
broken, and the round shiny bulb at the bottom looked
so bright, she decided to put it in her sack, you never
knew, it might come in useful somehow. By now it was
getting dark, she could hardly see, even if there had
been any more treasures. But away in the distance she
saw a little fire burning, and heard children's voices.
Curious, she wandered towards them and stood in the
shadows, watching. She saw that they had found an
old iron ladle and were heating something in the flames.
Presently they took the ladle off the fire and tipped its
contents out into a battered old basin full of water.
She heard a sizzling sound and saw clouds of steam as
the children all crowded round the basin in tense excitement. What on earth were they doing? Suddenly
she remembered—"Of course, it's All Hallows' E'en.
They're telling their fortunes with melted lead"! She
must have said this aloud, for the children looked up
startled, the firelight flickering on their faces. "Shall
we tell yours?" they said. She nodded and came to

77

crouch with them over the fire, watching while they put some more lead in the ladle and held it over the flames. "What you got in that bag?" they said, for she had put the sack carefully down beside her. "Oh, just bits of things," she answered, and one of the boys began blowing the fire till it roared. She peered into the ladle and saw the dull lumps begin to swim together into a little shiny lake. "Now!" said the children, and whisking the ladle over to the basin, they poured the molten lead into the water. "What is it?" they asked breathlessly, as it set in a curious shaped lump. "It's an x," said one. "No, it isn't, it's a flower with four petals," said another. "No, no, it's a flying bird!" They turned to her. "What d'you think it is?" She shook her head. Then the children picked the lump out of the water and gave it to her saying: "We don't know what it means, but you must take it, it will give you luck." So she thanked them, and swinging her sack on to her shoulder, went off into the darkness. She'd been so absorbed, she'd for a moment forgotten her fish's formula. But suddenly she thought, "Lead! Why, of course, number five!" Now there was only gold left, and the seventh that she had not thought of yet. But gold, how was she to find it, people did not leave that lying about in rubbish heaps. And she had no rings or brooches at home, she had long ago sold anything of that kind. She wandered on through the dark streets, racking her brains to think what do do. Presently she was pulled out of her thoughts by the sound of angry voices. A man and a woman, both in evening dress, were quarrelling on a doorstep. She could not hear what they said, but suddenly the woman burst into furious tears, and pulling something off her finger, hurled it out into the dark street. It rolled a long way and then finally fell into a muddy puddle close by the little old woman's feet. She waited a moment, saw that the couple were too busy quarrelling to notice her, then quickly picked it up and put it in her bag. What a bit of luck! It was a gold wedding ring. Number six! But as for the seventh, she did not even know what it was, much less where to find it. There was nothing for it but to wait and hope that something might turn up, so she set off down the street again. Then she remembered the broken thermometer. For her sack was feeling a bit heavy by now, and she thought she had better throw the thermometer away, as she did not really know why she had ever picked it up. She put down the sack and pulled it out from amongst the old tin cans, but as she did so the glass bulb hit against something and broke, so that all the quicksilver ran out and fell into one of the tins in a thousand bright balls. Quicksilver, quickSILVER, surely that must be a kind of metal! How silly of her not to think of that before! Now she had her seven metals at last. But goodness, what was she thinking of, it was long past the time when she ought to have been at home, and here she was wandering with a dirty old sack and not the slightest idea where she had got to. Of course the thing to do would be to ask a policeman the way home. There was one under the lamp at the corner. "Please, can you tell me the ..." She stopped suddenly, for the life of her she couldn't remember where it was she did live. To hide her confusion she stammered: "Please, could you tell me the time?" "Eleven forty-five," said the policeman, and she hurried away as fast as she could. Here was a nice situation, only sevenpence in her purse and not able to remember where she lived. She now had a horror of the police, they might really think she was mad and put her in an asylum. Then she thought, probably it was still that tiresome dream again, if there was any way she could make the gong out of her seven metals, then perhaps she'd be able to go home again. But how? You'd need some sort of fire of course, to melt them. And a pot. She began to wander through the streets again, peering into dark corners in the hopes of finding something in which to heat the metals. After a time she noticed that the streets were quite still and deserted, but she had by now quite forgotten, not only where she lived, but even that she ought to go home. Then in the distance she saw two red lamps on the road and a little shadowy hut, black against the red glow of a watchman's fire. Walking close up to it, she peered in and saw the shape of the watchman, apparently asleep. And there beside the hut, was a great iron bowl, black like a witches' cauldron. It seemed too good to be true, here was all she wanted to hand. But what about the watchman, mightn't he wake up in the middle? She crept closer, almost into the hut, and she could now hear him snoring; then on the ground beside him, she saw an empty whisky bottle. "Well, that's all right," she thought, and quickly undid her sack. One by one she put her precious metals into the black pot, the horse-shoe, the tin with the little shining lake of mercury at the bottom, and the queer shaped lump of lead that the children had given her. Then, from her purse, she took out the six-pence, the penny, and finally the discarded wedding ring. Carefully she placed the pot on top of the watch-man's brazier and then sat down on the kerbstone to wait. After a little, all impatience, she got up and prodded in the pot with an old stick. There was a chink of one metal against another, but no sign of melting. "I sup-pose it isn't nearly hot enough," she sighed, but caught her breath in the middle as a sudden gust of wind nearly blew her hat off. "And now there's going to be a storm, and it will put the fire out." she moaned, as a distant muttering rumble caught her attention. But although the wind blew harder and harder, it did not rain, it only sent the dust scudding into corners and flapped the canvas walls of the hut like a loose sail. And as it blew, the fire got hotter and hotter, so that the little old woman could not bear to stand near enough to see what was happening in the pot. The air was full of scudding bits of paper and straw, and through the roar of the wind she heard every now and then a crash which might have been a falling tile. Suddenly some-thing struck her head and she fell in a crumpled heap and lay still.

'When she came to, the wind had completely dropped and the fire in the brazier had nearly burnt itself out. She got up stiffly and hobbled eagerly towards it. Peering into the pot she saw, no longer rusty tin cans and a horse shoe, but a beautiful disk of shiny metal.

AN EXPERIMENT IN LEISURE

With the old sack in her hands for fear of burning herself, she seized hold of the pot, and tipped the disk out on the road, where it fell with a musical deep ring. Then terrified lest the watchman should now be awake, she stuffed it into the sack and hurried off. After some minutes fast walking she stopped breathless, for there before her she suddenly saw the river. She saw the dark water sliding by and to the left she saw a medley of masts and funnels. Close by there was the dim shape of a ship alongside a jetty, and there seemed to be people stirring aboard her. Something struck her as familiar, she felt irresistibly drawn and her feet took her straight along the jetty. Every moment she expected to be stopped, for surely such a place was not open to the public. But although she felt afraid, no one stopped her and she could not stop herself. Finally she found herself under the shadow of the towering black hulk. She could see letters painted and vaguely tried to spell them out. A—L, what next? E, or was it B? ALEAT —that didn't sound right somehow . . . ALB—then ALBAT—she craned up in the dimness to see the last letters—R—O—S—S. ALBATROSS! Where had she heard that name? Something to do with the North? Albatross . . . but of course, it was the name of the boat carrying an expedition to the North Pole, and . . . of course, tomorrow was the 26th, the very day the expedition was due to sail—or so the papers said. To think that she should have the luck to see it, and all by chance too. She stood still and gazed, imagining all the preparations going on inside. Then she wandered along the jetty and in the dark nearly fell over the end of a companion-way. She glanced at the sloping pathway that she could just see leading straight on to the deck. It really was too tempting, she must just have a peep, no one would see her in the dark . . . She crept up, and in a minute was standing on the deck. Fancy being on a real exploring boat, with ropes everywhere and a thick tarry smell. Suddenly her childish delight faded, she felt faint and remembered she had had nothing to eat since breakfast. Unsteady she began to feel her way down an open stairway, hoping to find assistance from someone. But down below it was pitch dark and still; as she had no strength to climb the stair again she groped her way a little further and then collapsed on a heap of something soft.'

3

'The *Albatross* steamed northward, day after day. The sailors said: "Our stowaway will bring us luck." And they said the little old woman must have nine lives else how could she have lived till they found her, many days out to sea. But the captain scratched his head, for he could not turn aside and drop her anywhere, they were late in the season already. So she stayed, and mended socks, and put patches in trousers, and when one of them got a cold she rubbed his chest. And always, in the locker they gave her, she kept her old sack with the gong in it, and sometimes when alone she would take it out and look at it. She liked its shiny smoothness, but its shape puzzled her, she'd never seen a gong with a little boss in the middle like that—it was more like a barbarian shield really.

'The days went on and they gave her warm clothes to wear—men's ones of course, they had nothing else. Soon they began to see icebergs, and then they began to see ice—miles and miles of it. But although there was ice to be seen everywhere, it did not close round them, they did not have to leave their ship and take to sledges, as they had expected. The captain scratched his head again, for this was not according to the rules of geography. All the same it was very useful, they were much better off in their ship.

'Then a day came when the men on board who had big heads and wore glasses—the little old woman supposed they were scientists, they did none of the rough work of the ship—seemed to be getting busy. The ship had been brought to anchor beside a solid field of ice, and she saw that these men were preparing to land. She watched them carry their instruments down the companion-way and walk across the snow to a spot where they stopped and seemed to be very busy about something she could not see at all. Plucking up her courage, she asked one of the sailors what was happening. "Tikin' observations, I s'pose. This 'ere's wot they calls the Magnetic Pole." Breathless with excitement, she slipped away to her bunk. Taking the gong out of the locker she gave it a last polish, and then began to tie a string through the two holes she had been patiently boring through its rim with a tool she had stolen from the carpenter. For, she had thought, to make a gong ring nicely you must hang it from a string. Hardly able to speak for excitement, she waited till the evening. Then in the queer brilliance of the northern midnight, she crept stealthily on deck and managed to slip down the companion-way on to the empty snow. She was terrified of being seen, but something seemed to have blinded the eyes of the watch. And at last she reached the spot where the trampled snow told her that the scientists had set up their instruments. Breathlessly she took the gong from its sack and held it out at arm's length by the string. Suddenly her heart sank—"You fool," she thought, "you've got nothing to strike it with!" But before she could think what could be done, her ears caught a rhythmic hum beating into the stillness and seeming to come from over her head. She looked up and saw a white bird circling in great spirals far above her. Nearer and nearer it came, while she watched it motionless, but still holding up the gong. Then it suddenly swooped straight at the gleaming metal boss. Too taken by surprise to save it, the little old woman only heard the blow and the booming vibration that followed, seeming to spread round her in louder and louder circles of sound. She had only time to see the beautiful white bird lying broken-necked at her feet before the spreading roar broke in a crash like thunder that seemed to shake the stars. She felt her feet sway under her and then came a tearing sound of breaking ice and she knew no more.'

4

'The day that the Polar expedition in the *Albatross* was due to reach the Magnetic North, there happened the worst earthquake that had ever been known. Ports and seaside places were engulfed in tidal waves,

85

and in the cities sky-scrapers rocked and some of them crumpled up. It was like a great shudder through the earth, as if an electric shock had passed through the veins in its body, the veins of lead and tin and iron and copper and gold and silver and mercury. And the instruments in the cities recorded that the centre of the disturbance was the Magnetic Pole. At sea there were the worst storms that any man remembered, and ships were tossed about like bits of cork, till some of them foundered and sank in mid-ocean and some were pounded to bits against the shores.

'After the storms had died down relief ships were sent out to bring help to the inundated cities; one of these reported that a new island had mysteriously appeared in the middle of the Pacific. In fact the whole thing was rather mysterious, for they had sent a boat ashore on this small spot of land not marked on their charts, and found it was a heap of rock and mud covered with curious sea-weeds now drying in the sun, and entangled amongst them parts of the bodies of queer-shaped bony fishes and unfamiliar shells. There was not a blade of grass or any sign of fresh water, indeed it seemed as though the whole place might have just been flung up from the bottom of the sea. And the odd thing was that on the highest point, they found a curious bronze mummy. It was like a great metallic cocoon, as big as a man, looking as though it had been woven from bronze silken threads, but when you touched it, it was hard as iron, as if some tremendous pressure had hardened it round a living chrysalis. And on one side of it was smeared some dark writing—"THE DEATH'S

HEAD EMPEROR." ... They thought this must be the work of a sailor whose body they found close by, only recently dead, probably a castaway from one of the wrecks. He must have become delirious from thirst and exposure and in his madness cut his own artery to christen the metal mummy in blood.'

CHAPTER SEVEN

MY first thought was that this was nothing but 'a tale told by an idiot, full of sound and fury, signifying nothing'. But was the mind an idiot when left to itself, without conscious reasoning? I knew only too well that it seemed so, for my usual day-dreams were sufficiently futile; but this story was not like a usual day-dream. The only way to test the matter was to see whether the images used had any relation to my real experience. Before doing this however, I had to ask myself why I could not finish the story, for I remembered that up till the end the images unfolded themselves without difficulty; but then it was as if I had come to a fork in the road and did not know which way to take, for two conflicting images struggled against each other. There seemed little difficulty about how the metal cocoon was to be opened, but the trouble was, what was going to come out of it? I saw seeds dropped on the island by birds and beginning to grow, till finally plants covered the bronze cocoon. And gradually the juices of their clinging roots and the fresh water of rain softened the great metal shell, until it began to crumble, and then movement had begun, small upheavings, as from something inside trying to get out. But the figure that finally burst out was not clear to me, it was like two photographs taken one on top of the other; one, the beautiful gentle spring god, Adonis; the other a dark warrior, brazen-helmeted and armed with shining weapons. And as I watched, the dark warrior grew to a whole army like himself, like the armies from the dragon's teeth of legend, rank upon rank, hard and darkly gleaming in the sun.

Still I could not decide which it was to be, so I went on to consider what ideas were connected with other parts of the story. The first thought that appeared was about the feathers that the little fishes brought to clothe their plaything with:

'. . . Those parrot's feathers that my father gave me once, out of that chest he had full of bright feathers and coloured silks for making fishing flies, the colours of that old salmon fly, and the smell of the beeswaxed thread when he was making them—then that little cedar-wood box I kept my treasures in, the Indian beetle, green and red and gold with a purple sheen on him—taking the box to boarding school and only opening it at night when the moonlight shone on my bed, so that no one else should know about it—the smell of the cedar-wood —and the smell of the burning rose-leaves in that clay lamp I made . . .'

These had certainly been some of my playthings as a child. But had they failed me in the way that the feathers were no use to the little fishes? I remembered now how put out I had been when I had discovered that my father was not really very good at making flies, he liked the idea of it but he was very clumsy with his fingers. And with that thought came the memory of how when I had turned away from delight in matters

89

of imagination and taken up science, my father had said: "I don't like your science, I want to keep my illusions."

Then I thought of the echoes of geography lessons that had come into the story, the deep pits in the Pacific Ocean with phosphorescent fishes, the Magnetic North, the muddy waters of the Amazon. The old woman's search for metals made me think at once of learning chemistry, and the phrase "Death's Head Emperor" brought back the days when I collected moths and butterflies, the smell of the cyanide killing bottle, and how I found a huge bronze cocoon and chrysalis that I thought should be an Emperor moth and had kept it hopefully all through one winter, but there had only hatched out a large Yellow Underwing; and there was also the Death's Head moth, which I never found but always hopefully looked for.

Of course, it was quite to be expected that in writing a fairy story one would use images from childhood, but did the story have any further importance for me? I could not see how it should and yet the feeling of importance still clung to it. What was this plaything, this skeleton that had to be clothed and brought up from the five-mile depths and which, when it did come up, was either loving or fierce, I did not know which?

With the question there now came into my head the general problem which my wanderings had brought me to just before I remembered to look at my fairy tale: the problem of the connection between the ID, Nature as a blind destroying force, and my Inner Fact. Was it possible that this was what my fairy tale was about, that actually all my life I had been hunting for my play-mate, continually seeking to come close to "the other", to all that was not me, and yet continually thwarted in the search by my opposing ideas of it, opposing feelings of love and terror? And was not this "other" also something which I felt stirring within myself, impulses which made me feel "this is none of I"? Was this further evidence that the solitary delights of childhood were attempts to clothe and bring into daylight this dim sense of the self by which I was lived, and which I also saw continually reflected in the growing things of earth? But why the five-mile depths? Here I remembered my feeling of the dumbness of flesh in the big animals at the Zoo. Was it simply the weight of the æons of blind living behind me that I was struggling against? Or was it, as I thought Freud would say, the crudeness of my first infantile ideas of "the other", a crudeness that made them too terrifying to be brought anywhere near the surface and the daylight?

And then, also, what about later loves, when I had given up childish play? I began to wonder whether the problem at the end of the fairy tale did not also account for some of the stresses of falling in love. On looking back it occurred to me that I had chosen to fall in love with those people who, I thought, combined the two aspects, people that I thought, though often mistakenly, could be both fierce and gentle. Only later had I discovered the futility of hoping to find the solution to one's own problems all ready-made in another person, on whose wonderful qualities one could live parasitically for ever.

AN EXPERIMENT IN LEISURE

But before I understood this, it had often puzzled me that the people I had temporarily fallen in love with had nearly always been disapproved of by my friends. Was it the witchcraft theme again? Was it also a clue to the problem of the beast within, was it that I had not yet faced the fact of destroying nature within, as well as outside, and that the impulse to face ˙it drove me on to find it in other people? I had often noticed among women that those who had above all been brought up to be "nice", who by long training were continually gentle and considerate, were just those who tended to fall in love with men who were ruthless.

Once, when these thoughts were beginning to stir in my mind, I had found myself buying a railway ticket next to a perfect stranger who had caught my attention with a shock of interest. Suddenly I had decided to follow the clue, no matter through what difficulties, and find what it might mean. In my diary I find these notes:

> . . . I saw your dark hair and profile as you stood in front of me buying your ticket. In the train you came along and helped me open the window, but again I did not see you full face. Then you walked along the corridor and our eyes met and I saw bitterness and despair there. But later in the bus I heard you talk happily and easily with strangers and heard you laugh. And when our routes parted you smiled at me, although we had not spoken at all, and your eyes were now friendly. . . .
>
> Then when we sat in the café (you were so late, what sort of a fool was I to have waited!) you told me of a novel you wanted to write and the plot was full of bitterness.

CHAPTER SEVEN

When we parted there was nothing, and I still was not sure what it was I had wanted.

What I took at first to be the failure of this experiment had plunged me into despair at the time, for I thought it showed that the feeling of allurement must be only a will-o'-the-wisp leading me nowhere. At first I had thought it made Keats's one certainty—the holiness of the heart's affections—seem a lie; but later I came to see that though the heart's affections certainly might not seem to be holy, the guess that they might contain a wisdom of their own was not quite disproved by this experiment. For I thought I had seen a certain frank ruthlessness, and I thought now that it was ruthlessness that I had wanted.

Gradually it occurred to me that here, perhaps, had been an example of a natural law of compensation working itself out. Just in so far as I had, all my life, accepted other people's standards, done what I had done in order to be the kind of person parents and friends would approve of, just so far would I have to find some way of adjusting the balance. For it was certain that, as a child, I had come to feel that not to be what those I loved expected of me was a matter of eternal damnation—disapproval, a "row" from them was something that I had felt utterly destroyed my being, and I had lived in continual dread of it. So all those natural impulses that happened not to be approved of by adults were stifled before I even knew they existed. But that was not the end of them, for here was I finding this lost part of myself continually beckoning to me with irresistible force in those who had lived in the opposite way, and chosen to defy approval. For a long time I had guessed that the difficulties of the "good" child were just as serious as those of the "bad" child, perhaps more so. For as a "good" child, I had never learnt not to mind hurting or displeasing and so had never accepted my own power to hurt or realized that to please everyone is spiritual death.

Was this then, perhaps, one of the things that I had had to bring up from the five-mile depths, the power to destroy, a power that is in everyone and that I had persistently denied in myself? Was it this that I had labelled the "Death's Head Emperor", the symbol of violence and defiance? Was the possibility of this fact in myself something that had to be accepted and digested before I could trust myself to the self in me that was not clear-headed purpose and reasoning? Had I felt this destroying power in myself and therefore also in the world around me, as a continual threat, and was this partly why I had found even physical relaxation so difficult?

In trying to catch the image of the armed power that seemed to be emerging in my fairy tale, I was reminded of Pluto, god of the under-world, whose other name was Dis. Then also I remembered Persephone whose story had had a curious power over me as a child.

One day it occurred to me that perhaps each person must for himself live through all the stages of the history of the gods, and that I was still the devotee of an older cult, my spirit still spent half her days in the gloom of the under-world, anxiously placating this dark destroying thing. But in the myth Persephone was never entirely freed. Would there, for me also, always be two antagonistic gods, always—Dis and Adonis? Was there no way by which one could come to grips with the beast within, break his dark domination and destroy his kingdom of fear? Surely there must be, for the story of Persephone and Dis was not the final word of mythology. But to come to grips with him one must know where to find him. And though, through symbolism, I could guess his nature, I could not tell in actual literal fact what I must do. I could only see the two-facedness of my god, see that dim Janus who was son of the bestial Hecate, but who nevertheless carried a bunch of keys and presided over the gates by which prayers ascend to the gods.

Then I remembered many-headed Cerberus, who also lived at the gate to the under-world, and how so often the heroes of myth had had to begin their adventures with slaying a monster. Was this the way to reconcile God and the Devil, to bridge the gap between Heaven and Hell? And if it was, what exactly had they done in these fights? What exactly was the dragon? And where was the critical point where it could be vanquished? I thought over all the dragon killings that I could remember, but found no clue. Then, in an old alchemical parable, I came across an account of a similar fight with a beast that interested me very much:

"They led me to the lion and described him very carefully, but what I should undertake with him none could tell me. Some of them indeed hinted, but very darkly, so

95

that the Thousandth one could not have understood him. But when I should first succeed in subduing him and should have assured myself against his sharp claws, and keen teeth, then they would conceal nothing from me. Now the lion was very old, ferocious and large, his yellow hair hung over his neck, he appeared quite unconquerable, so that I was almost afraid of my own temerity and would gladly have turned back if my promise and also the circumstance that the elders stood about me and were waiting to see what I would do, had allowed me to give up. In great confidence I approached the lion in his den and began to caress him, but he looked at me so fiercely with his brightly shining eyes that I could hardly restrain my tears. Just then I remembered that I had learned from one of the elders, while we were going to the lion's den, that very many people had undertaken to overcome the lion and very few could accomplish it. I was unwilling to be disgraced, and I recalled several grips that I had learned with great diligence in athletics, besides which I was well versed in natural magic, so I gave up the caresses and seized the lion so dexterously, artfully and subtly, that before he was well aware of it I forced the blood out of his body, yea, even out of his heart. It was beautifully red but very choleric. I dissected him further and found, a fact which caused me much wonder, that his bones were white as snow and there was much more bone than there was blood." [1]

There was much detail here that I did not understand at all, but there was one item which I found bore upon my problem of the moment, and that was the magical grip by which the hero overcomes the lion where others had failed. For a long time I wondered

[1] Herbert Silberer: *Problems of Mysticism and its Symbolism*, pp. 3–4.

what this might be, and then I find the following note in my diary:

> June 6. Critical point. I woke at 4 a.m. and became lost in a reverie, felt I should write it down but couldn't pull myself out of the lovely bodily lassitude enough to do it. Suddenly it occurred to me that somehow this might be the critical point, for me at least, the moment of pulling oneself to the effort of deliberate expression—that this might be the magical grip on the lion that cannot be tamed by caress and gentle words. For I had remembered F. on Sunday, when she had J.H. (aged two) on her knee and said: "He's such a bully!"—with that open-mouthed guffaw of hers—and he climbed over her and she exulted in it, in spite of all her troubles—him and her —it did not matter that the tea-party was not a success, no social brightness and ease of conversation—here was something else—I thought of this wildness in her, the primitive possessiveness, fierce possessiveness of J., fierce domination of others, and now I liked it. For suddenly I felt the truth of her as raw experience, felt it as an intense moment of significance, felt my consciousness or whatever it is gathered to a focus and crashing down like a hammer on an anvil, banging the red-hot moment into shape, catching the present moment, the only moment in which action is possible, usually its power dissipated in clouds of past and future, but this present instant a clanging thing, sending out sparks—and other moments of raw experience which can somehow be fished out of the depths of the past and revived, brought back to that live actuality —like the live dormouse in my hand . . . raw experience, the crash of hammer on iron.

I had written this in the middle of the night and it had seemed to me very important. But in the morning I was not at all sure what it meant. Was the feeling about it only one of those "delusions of grandeur", as when the thing you were just going to say but have forgotten seems of such intense importance? I thought not, on the whole, for the images had a greater power over me now than when I had written them, even though I could not say in logical terms just what they meant. I thought:

'. . . unformulated experience, that is, nature in the raw, nature shut off from awareness, is this the dragon? But isn't nature—that is, human nature, as one feels it in oneself—isn't it desires? Desires without the integrating power of awareness, is this then the destroying dragon? But to become aware of a desire you must somehow let go wanting the thing and simply look—is this the "magical grip"?'

August Bank holiday. I've been reading the Tao Te Ching [1] and brooding over the Quietist "desirelessness". When I first heard of it, it seemed so impossible, so lifeless, as if one only lived in one's desires. But now, letting them go by an internal gesture, this seems to be the act of sacrifice which must be continually repeated if awareness is to grow—a mysterious act that has a fertilizing effect.

Had then this darkly gleaming image, that fought for place with the life-giving Adonis, brought me back once more to the internal gesture of giving up all purposes, that I had called the fire-sacrifice? Was this the way to deal, not only with the fear of power without, but also with the the fear of power within, fears which

[1] Lao Tze

apparently could cast shadows of gloom over me? Was this dark image at one and the same time a reflection of my own hidden desire to dominate and hurt and also a direct means of satisfying the desire to be dominated and hurt, so that I actually sought out people in whom I could glimpse a like Satanic vein? And had I not already guessed that if one did not satisfy this dark desire for surrender of the will in a ritual sacrifice, it would find its own way out, the ID would drive one's spirit continually into the dismal under-world of the Death's Head Emperor? Was it only by the death of Adonis that I could escape the domination of Dis?

In my head was ringing, although I had not thought of it at all when writing the fairy story:

> "Full fathom five thy father lies;
> Of his bones are coral made;
> Those are pearls that were his eyes:
> Nothing of him that doth fade,
> But doth suffer a sea-change
> Into something rich and strange."

CHAPTER EIGHT

SINCE I had observed that a new fact must dawn on me many times before I had any permanent hold upon it, I find it very difficult to trace the development of my discoveries with any accurate order of time. So now I must describe something which happened much earlier than the ideas of the last chapter, but I had not been able to see any meaning in it till now.

Shortly after finishing the account of my first floundering attempts to find out what I wanted,[1] I had been to see Sean O'Casey's play "Within the Gates". I had enjoyed the performance, but was afterwards haunted by it and puzzled. For in addition to the moment to moment interest in the acting, I thought the author was saying something important, but at the time I could not tell what this might be. When I got home I thought I could perhaps find a clue if I tried writing down a summary of the action of the play:

'It is the story of a young prostitute called Janice, illegitimate child of a drunken mother, who had run away from her mother's violence. The scene is in a corner of a public park and when the girl first appears she is having trouble with her heart and is in terror of living alone. She appeals to various people for help;

[1] *A Life of One's Own.* Published by Macmillan & Co., 1934.

first, an Atheist platform speaker, who had partially adopted her as a child, and she pleads that he should again make a home for her. But he says she must live her own life. Then she appeals to a gardener who has been one of her lovers, that he should marry her. But he makes excuses and her urgent entreaties are observed by a policewoman, so that she is given a month's imprisonment for soliciting. When she comes out her heart is worse and she is more frightened still; she appeals to a bishop, who has been hanging about the park "trying to get in touch with the common people". But he only listens coldly, giving conventional and pious advice. Then she meets a young poet with a windfall of money and goes off with him, but when the money is all spent she is back again in the park, her heart attacks worse than ever. The bishop now offers help, suggesting that he could get her into the hostel of a pious sisterhood, but she meets this suggestion with vicious ribaldry, breaking into a gay song and dance. In the middle of it is heard a mournful chant and monotonous drum-beat, and all who hear it—two chair attendants who have just lost their jobs, two evangelists, and the prostitute herself—stiffen, intently listening. The chant comes nearer and nearer while everything darkens and grows chilly. Then grey figures begin to file slowly past, hopeless wrecks of old and young, chanting miserably. Although left dejected by these apparitions, the prostitute again refuses the bishop's offer; but she is still in dire need, and when a Salvation Army group begins to hold a service close by, she listens and becomes emotionally stirred, finally running into the group to kneel before the officer. Just as she is about to be accepted as a repentant sinner, the poet appears, saying he has money again, and calls her away to "another month of gay and crowded life, of wine and laughter".

'In the last scene she appears with the poet once more, but even paler, and with a fixed look of fear. The poet fails to comfort her and she demands that he find the bishop. The drum-beat of the chant of the Down-and-Outs is heard again, and as they file in they begin to close around her, the poet vainly trying to encourage her to defiance. She falls to the ground, but as she dies, calls to the bishop to help her make the sign of the cross.'

This is the barest outline of the action of the play and gives no hint of its quality. For there is a continual coming and going in the park, flirtatious nursemaids, a guardsman, argumentative stragglers from the platform speakers' groups, two evangelists and the prostitute's drunken old mother, coming and going with a rhythm that reminded me of ballet. There are also deliciously realistic, although slightly burlesqued, conversations between the nursemaids and their lovers, the chair attendants, the platform speakers and their hangers-on. Then, in addition to the chanting procession of the Down-and-Outs, other non-realistic techniques are used: a boy, having pestered his nurse to know what "Community Singing" means, gets the answer, "the singin' of songs by the community at large". And after his question, "What's the community at large, Nannie?" there come in, "from the right and from the left variously, the Foreman, the Man with the Bowler Hat, a Man in Shorts, the Man with the Stick, and others . . ." They sit in a row on chairs and each with conventionalized movements unfolds a newspaper. They hold the papers so that a page appears before each reader like a placard. On one paper is the word "Murder", on another "Rape", on others "Divorce", "Racing", "Suicide", "Execution", and "Great Cricketer talks about God". After a few moments a gramophone is heard playing "London Bridge is Falling Down". The second verse is reached:

"Gold and silver will not do, will not do, will not do;
Gold and silver will not do, my fair lady."

And during this the readers have looked up angrily over the tops of their papers to where the gramophone is playing. Then the prostitute appears and joins in the singing in a jaunty way, moving among the readers, "rustling their precious papers and disturbing their peace". She surveys them thoughtfully for a few moments, then "ironically lifting her hand in a gesture for silent reverence" begins: "Hush, hush, the oblate brothers are busy reading the gospel for the day. Sucking in holy thoughts of holy wisdom. Let us pray. Oh, Lucifer, Lucifer, who has caused all newspapers, stars of the morning and stars of the evening, to be written for our learning, grant that we may so read that we may always find punch in them, hot stuff in them, and sound tips in them, so that both outwardly in our bodies, and inwardly in our souls, we may get closer and closer to Thee! . . . Why the Hell don't you all say Amen?" They take no notice of her and after a few remarks to the bishop, who tries to make her come away, she begins again, recklessly: "I've had a few drinks, but what about it? A short life and a merry one! My heart's due to stop beating any time now, but what about it?" She contemplates the readers: "Devoted, body and soul, to the love of learning. Janice's going to die dancing." Vehemently: "Are all you damn perishers deaf and dumb?" And the readers answer, chanting in chorus:

"We want to read, want to read, want to read in peace."

Then she begins to sing again, recklessly, but becomes breathless, and presses her hand to her side: "I'm a sick woman . . . Death has touched me, and is telling me to be ready; take your things off and come with me." Defiantly: "I'll not give in, I'll not hold back. And when I go, should God's angels beckon me up or push me down, I'll go game." Horrified: "Jesus, Son of Mary, what'm I saying? I'll fold all the things done in this life round me like a mantle, and wait for judgment."

She sinks down on a seat, but the readers still take no notice and in turn read out lurid extracts from their papers. When they have finished she begins to taunt them again: "What are you all seeking? You look like a silent gang of monkeys searching for fleas. . . . Is there no one far enough from the way of the world to take an interval of rest and have a look at me?" and she begins to dance. "Now you deaf and dumb perishers, have a look at a lovely pair of legs, if you're not blind as well." And now they all look over the tops of their papers and watch her. But when she sinks down, pale and breathless, they all go back to their papers again and take no notice when she gasps out: "I can't breathe, I can't breathe. It's on me again, but I'll go game, I'll go game. Eyes front, up or down." In a panic of fear: "Dance, sing and strip for the fun of the thing—that's all they want from a woman. A sigh, a sob of pain, a thought higher than their own from a woman, and they're all hurrying home . . . God damn you, will none of you stir to help when you see a Christian in danger?"

What puzzled me at first was that the main characters were not realistic at all. No prostitute ever talked such poetry, or certainly not in England, and since the other characters talked good Cockney it was surely meant to be an English park. And no bishop was surely ever quite so fatuously pious and jovial as this one was at the beginning. In fact, I was reminded of those old morality plays in which the characters were not intended to be real people at all, but symbols of qualities. Their speech also had none of the rhythm of ordinary conversation; I almost thought at times it was rhymed, for one answered another, not with logical answers, but with a musical repetition of sounds.

But I thought: Am I now any nearer knowing why O'Casey wrote this play? Has he merely used a clever formalized and poetic technique to convey a picture of modern life as he sees it? Has he anything definite to say about what he sees? He has said that fear of losing one's job and becoming destitute haunts the poor; he has said that a prostitute's life is precarious, that orators argue on matters they know nothing about and that the majority of people are hungrily absorbed in seeking after sensation. But those are things that everybody knows; he has certainly said them picturesquely but he has said nothing new about them. . . . It cannot be these truisms that make the play seem so important. Can the point of it perhaps lie in the desolate murmur of the drunken old woman who wanders about putting poppy wreaths on War Memorials, mourning the memory of a dead dragoon who was her husband for only a week before he left for the Front: "Your politics are husks that only swine will eat; your power's behind a battlement of hunger; your religion's as holy as a coloured garter round a whore's thigh; truth's bent in two and hope is broken. O Jesu, is there no wisdom to be found anywhere? . . ." Certainly this was a recurrent theme in the play; the first impression it left was that all is futility.

But was that all? It occurred to me to wonder whether, under the guise of talking about the futilities of modern life, he wasn't really perhaps talking about something quite different, not talking about the outer struggle for a livelihood and safety, but about an inner struggle—just as in the morality plays? I thought that hints of this were given in the title and in the fact that the young poet in the play is called the Dreamer: when the curtain rises two great shut gates are seen, and the Dreamer walks up from the audience to pass through them. Obviously these were not merely the gates of a park, he was also opening a way into his own mind, as into a dream. If so, the characters in the play, as so often in a dream, might be, not pictures from life, but symbols of different aspects of the Dreamer's own personality. With this in mind I thought it might be worth while to analyse the various characters and themes and try to see what they might stand for.

One of the most obvious themes was physical sexuality: the nursemaids with their lovers; the gardener who, while he works, day-dreams of the girl he will sleep with at night; the Man in Plus-fours who several times passes across the stage silently pursuing the Scarlet Woman; the prostitute's gay life with the Dreamer himself and the story of how she lost her job because she would not let her employer make love to her. And linked with this there was a recurrent theme of sterility: there was the sterile respectability of the bishop's sister; the sterile religiosity of the bishop who has nothing to give them even when he does "get in touch with the common people"; the sterile sensuality of the gardener who refuses the responsibility of marrying; the sterile intellectual arguments of the platform speakers who never reach wisdom; the prostitute who longs to have a child but cannot find anyone to give her the kind of life that would make it possible—and her drunken mother, mourning the dead dragoon "and the golden infancy of England's life".

But if sterility was one of the themes, so also was fear. I thought of the prostitute's cry to her adopted father: "When I lie down in bed and stretch out in search of sleep, the darkness reddens into a glow from the fire that can never be quenched"—and I could not help remembering *Pilgrim's Progress* and Christian's terrors of fire. She is also terrified of death, but is at the same time defiant of it, for when her heart attacks or the sound of the chant of the Down-and-Outs makes her think of death she declaims: "I'll go game, I'll die dancing." And in the end it is the bishop who tries to overcome her defiance. When she appeals to him for help against the approaching Down-and-Outs with: "Let me not mingle my last moments with this marching misery!" he answers: "You must go where they go, and their sighing shall be your song. You must mingle your last hour with the dust that marching life has left behind her." And the Down-and-Outs chant:

> "You must be merry no more; you must walk in the midst
> of the mournful;
> Who've but a sigh for a song, and a deep sigh for a drum-
> beat."

But it is the Dreamer who tries to prevent her, who encourages her to continued defiance with: "Sing them silent; dance them still; laugh them into an open shame!" And it is he who, after the prostitute dies, answers the Down-and-Outs' chant with:

> "Way for the strong and the swift and the fearless:
> Life that is stirred with the fear of its life, let it die;
> Let it sink down, let it die, and pass from our vision for
> ever."

What interested me especially here was the linking of the two themes, fear of loss and poverty and death, with the idea of sterility. Immediately the thought of fertility rites cropped up again in my mind and with it, images from T. S. Eliot's *Waste Land*. 'Surely', I thought, 'isn't "Within the Gates" really dealing with the same theme?' In the old ceremonies the women wept for the death of Adonis, here the drunken mother of the prostitute weeps for her dead dragoon; in the old ceremonies it was the winter death of flowers and grass and leaves that they wept for under the name of Adonis, here the sterility is not of the land but of the people: futile argument, futile sensationalism, futile promiscuity—and also futile poetry, for it had struck me at once how all the utterances of the character called 'The Dreamer' (who was also supposed to be a poet) somehow rang false, culminating in his final remark to the dying prostitute: "Fear nothing; God will find room for one scarlet blossom among His thousand white lilies." But then it was also this Dreamer who identified himself with "the strong and the swift and the fearless". Was it not possible that the writer of the play was really dealing again with the Odysseus-Telemachus contrast? Then the Dreamer and the Prostitute would be the two sides of himself, and the Prostitute would stand for his sense of his own weakness, for the part of his mind that was receptive and therefore continually possessed by others; his poetic imagination had leapt ahead and shown him the need to embrace inner poverty, but he had also experienced its tremendous difficulty. He had seen the need to cast Adonis into the waters, but had not been able to do it, at least not until the very last moment of the play, when the Prostitute dies making the sign of the cross. I wondered, did the writer believe in the end of the Adonis ritual, the resurrection of the dead? Having linked sterility with fear of dying, did he then go on to suggest that fertility came from acceptance of death? I thought not, for I remembered that it was at the beginning, not the end of the play, that all who were wandering through the park sang:

> "Our mother, the earth, is a maiden again,
> Young, fair, and a maiden again.
> Her thoughts are a dance as she seeks out her bride-
> groom, the sun,
> Through the lovely confusion of singing of birds, and of
> blossom and bud."

Whether all this was the "true" interpretation of the play or not, was no concern of mine; I thought there might be several other versions—for instance, the purely psycho-analytic one, or the author's own account of what he meant, which I thought would most likely be quite different from the one I had given. But this did not worry me, since my sole concern at the moment was to borrow forms, no matter from where, by means of which my own obscure preoccupations could declare themselves.

CHAPTER NINE

On looking back through my diary I found the description of another experience which had made a deep impression and which had forced me again to consider the question of the impulse to submit.

It was soon after seeing "Within the Gates" and I was planning to go abroad. Written during the days before starting, I find various notes in my diary—at the time, I had written them blindly, simply to gain relief from a mood, but I now saw that they had a definite bearing upon what followed:

> . . . For days I have been haunted by the anxieties of illness, of A. and M. and G., and F.'s mother, all ill . . . and also thoughts of political brutalities . . .
>
> . . . at the Zoo, crossing the canal bridge, screams and squeaks and monkey whistles, what is there about those parrots high up in the dim space of the aviary? . . . those sea-lions: what marvellous abandon to water and the movement of their bodies. . . . In the big aviary, those gulls and herons and long-legged things which all soared off to crowd round the little girl with buns, drawn, as if by a magnet, to fill their bellies—like human migrations, herdsmen following the grass, young men from villages flocking to the towns—and then the fat smug oily stupidity of those penguins, seeing nothing beyond themselves, flat-footed and pompous.
>
> March 13th. . . . still haunted by the thought of

AN EXPERIMENT IN LEISURE

M.'s worries over A.'s illness, and forebodings about Fascism.

19th. What is this sudden memory of a bridge over water, the bridge at Guildford over the backwater from the weir where I tried to fish as a child—but my line was not long enough to reach the water, low water, shallow, not the main stream . . . And then that great empty river of sand in Oklahoma, where we looked for depths and a cool bathe, but it was barely above our knees.

20th. D.R. came in to tea yesterday—I said "There are so many people ill and dying." She said: "Isn't that a good thing?" most cheerfully.

Then I had set out on my journey, and once more tried to record whatever especially caught my attention, odd sights or sounds, little glimpses of landscape or people:

. . . That gendarme on the quay at Dieppe, brutal looking, when a boy ventured near the boat, he strode up and hustled him back. I felt full of anxiety towards this brutal power of Authority.

That old woman I saw from the train in the foot-hills of the Pyrenees, padding home with such determination, leading her cow.

In the cathedral at Easter, all the patient crowd at High Mass, and those arrogant fat-robed bishops and priests— like penguins.

Conversation overheard.

HE (*having had a nervous breakdown*): "If I was an artist I wouldn't know what to do, with so many different schools and theories, I wouldn't know what to paint, how to paint."

SHE (*who made a lot of money by it*): "But you'd know from the heart."

CHAPTER NINE

HE. "I feel it's a waste of time because my paintings are not worth anything afterwards."

Most of the following weeks were spent in simple physical pleasures, walking, dancing, sailing, swimming, but wherever I went I found myself deeply drawn towards the houses and occupations of the poor —an old bare-footed peasant woman, a herdsman with goats, the little snatches of song from those tilling the fields, groups chatting round doorsteps in the evening. I never wanted to see any famous architecture or historic buildings, and when one day they said: "In that great cleft in the mountains is the last stronghold of the Moors—will you come with us to see it?" I did not go but remained staring at the gap in the mountains.

Then, slowly growing through the drifting plans of my holiday, came the determination to see a bull-fight. I had heard someone talk about bull-fighting in a bus —I had scraped an acquaintance with him, in order to find out how I could see one and the best time and place. I rearranged my plans accordingly and set out to see a day of famous fighters, having received a final warning—"Remember it is *not* a sport, but a sort of Russian Ballet with Death for its theme."

Afterwards I tried to write an account of the fight. But when I tried to remember exactly what had happened I found my mind hovering round the thought of something quite different, I remembered looking at the Pyrenees from the Paris express the morning after, a cold wet morning when some sudden lift in the clouds showed a range of mountains covered with fresh snow and shining in the sun. And I remembered being helplessly seasick two nights before in the same storm that had covered the Pyrenees with fresh shining snow, and I remembered the seven Spanish women who were sick with me and two children who moaned. And again I remembered mountains, and how, many days before the fight I had read *Death in the Afternoon*,[1] and then whenever a view of mountains loomed into sight, there had also loomed the thought of bulls. And now with that memory, came finally a memory of the ring. But it was not a memory of any matador, it was a curious fused impression of two opposing moods, ringing together in my head like a complicated chord. I saw the grotesque and meaningless angle of a dead bull's head as it was hauled by the neck across the sand, dragged in triumph by a team of galloping horses that were gay with bells. And almost at the same time I saw the live bull at its first entrance, bewildered but challenging, such an intense focus of vitality that the very air of the ring quivered and grew tense from the moment he appeared. And I felt a monotonous repetition of these two pictures, neither of which could quite wipe out the other, a monotonous quality that reminded me that I had seen six bulls killed. And, for a moment freeing myself from this spell of monotony, it occurred to me that English friends had reported how they went to a bull fight and were really very interested, even in spite of the awful bit with the horses, but having seen one or two bulls killed they felt there was no point in staying till the end . . . But I thought you might as well cut a painting in half. Always—the living—and

[1] Hemingway.

114

the dead—the one following so quickly upon the other and with a relentless certainty like the ruthlessness of natural law. People say: "Oh, but I couldn't bear such lack of sportsmanship, the bull has no chance." Of course it hasn't, nor has the sun any chance to escape from setting nor summer leaves from shrivelling nor a man from dying.

I had come determined not to sympathize with the bull; enamoured of Spain I had reacted against all the shocked English talk of cruelty, and was full of thoughts of the matadors, of their superb control and audacity; I expected to be aware of the death which they continually avoided, not the death which the bull inevitably received. Of course Hemingway had mentioned that the whole thing was really the tragedy of the bull, but I did not want to think about that, and Hemingway himself gave far more attention to the skill of the matadors. But when it came actually to seeing a fight, it was quite different. I kept thinking: 'Oh, why can't they let him alone, all this cloak-flapping and showing off their cleverness!' But I did not really want it to stop; you might as well try to stop the playing of "King Lear" because you could not bear the pain of it. Some half-remembered line rang in my head . . . 'the gods . . . they kill us for their sport'. But however shocking to admit it, I had no impulse to rush in and do good to the bull, to save him from the pain and to stop the sport of the gods. For the whole thing seemed lifted right out of the level of personal feeling. The matadors might be the gods of Olympus or Valhalla, but I, as spectator, had occasional glimpses of a detachment that seemed beyond either tormenting gods or suffering men. For to me it did seem that it was the suffering bull which was the really human thing, hemmed in by forces he could not understand, spending his superb energies in charges against the air. And in these moments of detached seeing I felt a curious exaltation, as if by being able to watch it dramatically played out, one was in that moment purged from the accumulated sense of one's own and other people's futilities.

Blasphemous as it may seem, I had come away feeling as though I had attended the most fully satisfying religious ceremony of my life. I remembered adolescent church-going and how I would often work myself up to holy feelings and love towards my neighbour, and then come home to an inevitable reaction in which I loved nobody and nothing and was filled with petty irritations.

But after the bull-fight there was no such reaction, I felt purged and fuller and wiser. I tried then to understand why, and to think what the meaning of the bull-fight might be, or at least why it had affected me so deeply. Certainly it had something to do with those preoccupations of the past months which had been an undercurrent in all my living, preoccupations with the renewed outburst of cruelty and assertive destroying power in the world, and also with illness and the lives of the poor. But I had not then followed up the interest in primitive religious rites, so did not at first see the connection with the gesture of inner poverty. At first I thought that all those hidden lusts which the psycho-analysts talk of, lust of power, to kill and destroy, and of self-abasement, to be killed and destroyed, surely these were satisfied in the bull-fight, by participation, as never before. But then I thought that even if this were true it did not explain everything; I still, in thinking of the bull-ring, had a haunting sense of its importance, this sense that I had learnt was not to be ignored, since as long as an experience haunted me, I knew there was still something I had not understood about it.

I wondered particularly why I had not felt any desire to defend the bull and stop the cruelty, whereas at other times I had so often been filled with rage against the destroying power of the strong. When I heard about political atrocities I often "saw red", I was filled with a desire to hit back, to destroy those who were the destroyers. Once I had seen Eisenstein's film "Thunder over Mexico", in which the rulers trample three peasant boys to death with horses, the boys being buried in the earth all but their heads, so that they could not even die fighting. As I watched a dull rage in me had grown to a fierce throbbing in my stomach and I had longed to murder and utterly destroy those triumphant horsemen—while at the same time I felt resentment against Eisenstein for so exploiting my emotions. But in the bull-fight there had been no such feelings. Was this perhaps because there had been an inevitability about the bull-fight; one knew from the start that there was no escape, while in the film there was no such sense of the inexorable march of events? By some lack, I suppose, in the story-teller's art, I had not been made to believe in the necessity of the tragedy; the story had seemed haphazard and disjointed, it was exciting and

117

beautifully photographed, but there was no shock of truth about it. But in the bull-fight, which was not a play at all, in the sense of a realistic portrayal of some aspect of life, there was yet an immense sense of reality and the inevitability of fact. Incidentally, I am told that the Spaniards actually call the act of plunging the sword into the bull "the moment of truth". Was this just an accident, or was it possible that this was what the Spaniards were acting out Sunday after Sunday in every city of Spain, that one final and inescapable truth of life, the certainty of death? Had they, somehow through those intuitions which shape a culture, made practical application of the truth that psycho-analysis has just been laboriously re-discovering, the truth that fears must be faced, not hidden away?

But what did this mean for me in my daily life? I thought of it in relation to those preoccupations with cruelty that had obsessed me of late:

'Everywhere on the posters "MASSACRE OF ABYSSINIANS"—and my heart sank as it does every time I go out in the streets these days, or look at a news-paper. Not long ago it was—"MACHINE-GUNS IN VIENNA". Now it is—"MASSACRE OF ABYS-SINIANS"—how that word "massacre" aches with pain and horror. This dead weight of foreboding over international affairs, feeling of the pain of the common people everywhere, poverty and oppression, surely something can be done, must be done, why don't they DO something, all these "leaders", politicians, what is the truth, what are they all getting at, surely there must be a common-sense way out, something you can

CHAPTER NINE

DO? . . . But what's the good of what I'm doing, of feeling continuously this dead weight of pain over the world's troubles? I feel certain somehow that it's a destructive pain, a fruitless struggling against the facts —and when I hate the conquerors so vehemently, isn't it like J. who, when he was three, said he'd cut up into little bits all the people who kill other people?—or those fierce defenders of animals who will beat a man who beats a dog? Of course it's very nice to think one is so sensitively philanthropic—the pride with which Mrs. B. said to me the other day, "Oh I can't bear to see an animal suffer", that gave me a clue—that horror of pain, and fighting pain with violence, both are destructive. For suddenly this morning I found I could accept the pain, the painful facts, I could make the internal gesture of opening my arms to the hurt, accept the knife in my heart, and that fruitless ache of horror stopped.'

Then I remembered how, when reading Hemingway's book before seeing the bull-fight, I had at first felt sick at his descriptions of the injuries to matadors. But to be sick is to get rid of something, so I supposed I was trying to get rid of the thought of the pain. I had had an impulse to skip this part of the book, but then thought what a one-sided picture of the life of a matador I would get. Instead, I had let the thought of the injury sink down into me, and immediately I had stopped feeling sick, and what I was reading about had become intensely more real.

I thought it was not so much the getting rid of the discomfort of the painful thought that mattered, it was that by this acceptance of it I had become imaginatively alive. I brooded over the implications of this.

'Is it possible that it is only by such an act that one can ever see the truth at all? As long as you are fighting against the pain you cannot understand what brought it about? It seems paradoxical, but is it only by abandoning all thought of doing anything to improve a situation, the utter acceptance of the experience, seeing nothing beyond it, that knowledge of how to surmount the difficulty grows? I've found this true in my own small affairs.—"The moment of truth."—Or rather, it isn't necessarily the immediate difficulty that becomes solved by accepting the pain of it, I certainly do not have a world-important idea about foreign affairs as a result of opening my heart to the thought of machine-guns in Vienna—but I'm beginning to be sure that I do have some idea, that the certain result of such an acceptance is an illumination, although maybe in a quite different field. But the queer part is that you mustn't accept *in order to* have a good idea—that kills the whole process; you must accept as if there were nothing beyond.'

I remembered also how, just before seeing the bullfight, I had been suffering an intense personal pain and insult to my pride. For days I had fought blindly for some way out; I was surging with impulses to hurt back where I had been hurt. Then suddenly one morning, perhaps from sheer exhaustion, I had stopped fighting the pain, and immediately I had been filled with a vivid sense of the problems of the person who had caused it. Certainly it was now difficult to avoid the conclusion

CHAPTER NINE

that the acceptance of the sword and plunge into nothingness really was the "moment of truth", that not only was it the way to vanquish looming fears, but also the indispensable condition for true fertility of the imaginative mind. But even if it was indispensable I still found it as difficult as ever; part of me wanted to feel myself being myself all the time, I wanted to be always the matador, in perfect mastery of the situation, wielding the sword.

CHAPTER TEN

BROODING over these things, I one day chanced to re-read Ibsen's *Peer Gynt*. At first I had no clear idea what it was all about, but simply enjoyed the obvious satire in it. But it had that haunting quality which was my sign-post so I felt I must settle down to study it further.

My first clue was given by Ibsen himself in his introduction:

> . . . "to make the matter intelligible I should have to write a whole book, and for that the time has not yet come. Everything that I have written has the closest possible connection with what I have lived through, even if it has not been my own personal experience; in every new poem or play I have aimed at my own spiritual emancipation and purification." [1]

Before I had had time to re-read it with this in mind I came across an interpretation of the play written by a psycho-analyst.[2] This maintained that it expressed what to this critic seemed to be the deepest kind of love, the love between a man and his mother. In these terms the end of the play, the return to Solveig, was simply the fulfilment of the wish to return to the idealized mother, to the comfort and security of her lap. As far as it went I thought this was probably true, but did it go far enough? Was this not perhaps

---

[1] *Peer Gynt*, Everyman Edition, p. viii.
[2] Groddeck: *Exploring the Unconscious*.

another case of meanings within meanings, the truth of one not necessarily ruling out the truth of another? For the speeches of the Button Moulder indicate quite clearly that Peer is not going back to Solveig merely for comfort and security, he is to go back to have a second chance to become the kind of person he ought to have been; and if he does not, he is not worth keeping as an individual person, he must be melted down again into the common stock of raw material. He must, metaphorically, go back to his mother in order to be reborn. And not only this, there are also many hints in the play about what was the kind of person he ought to have been. For although it is the urge to power that has dominated Peer's life, the determination to become Emperor of the world, Ibsen clearly represents this urge as one-sided; for when Peer is faced with the son born from his adventure with the troll woman, Ibsen makes the mother say: "Can't you see that he's lame in the shanks as you're lame in your mind?" But what then is the side of Peer that had not grown? Ibsen seemed to me to be plainly saying that it was the creative artistic side, so making a clear distinction between this and the desire for power, a distinction that Keats also made when he said:

> "Men of genius are as great as certain ethereal chemicals operating in the mass of neutral intellect—but they have not any individuality, any determined character. I would call the top and head of those who have a proper self, men of power." [1]

[1]*Life and Letters of John Keats*, Richard M. Houghton, Biblio Distribution Center.

AN EXPERIMENT IN LEISURE

That it is the poet in him that has been stunted is shown by the scene in which Peer returns to his native land as an old man, and wanders upon the heath; the threadballs sing to him:

"We are thoughts;
You should have thought us;
Little feet, to life
You should have brought us!

PEER GYNT (*stumbling*).

Threadballs!   You infernal rascals!
Are you tripping up your father?   (*Runs away.*)

WITHERED LEAVES (*flying before the wind*).

We are a watchword;
You should have used us!
Life, by your sloth,
Has been refused us.
By worms we're eaten
All up and down;
No fruit will have us
For spreading crown.

PEER GYNT.

Still, you have not been born for nothing;
Lie still, and you will serve for manure.

(*A sighing in the air.*)

We are songs;
You should have sung us!
In the depths of your heart
We lay and waited;
You called us not.
May your throat and voice
With poison rot!

124

CHAPTER TEN

PEER GYNT.

Poison yourselves, you silly doggerel!
Had I any time for verse and twaddle?"

Again, there is the side-light of the incident when Peer
once watches a boy cut off his finger to evade military
service, and Peer thinks to himself:

"Chopped it right off!—a precious finger!
And did it, too, as if he meant it.
Oho, I see! If one's not anxious
To serve His Gracious Majesty
That is the only way. So that's it!
They would have called him for the army,
But he, I see, would be exempted.
Still, to cut off——? To lose for ever——?
The thought, perhaps—the wish—the will—
Those I could understand; but really
To *do* the deed! Ah, no—that beats me!"

But later when he returns from his travels and listens
to the funeral oration of someone who may have been
this same boy, he hears a story of a humble life of
physical creativeness. The priest describes the character of the man:

" He wasn't rich, nor was he very clever;
His voice was weak, his bearing scarcely manly;
He had no strength of mind, nor much decision;
Nor in his own home did he seem the master.
His manner when he came to church was such
As if he felt he must request permission
To take his seat among the congregation."

But the priest goes on to tell how he had built and

rebuilt his farm, in spite of floods and avalanches, and successfully reared a family. The final judgment is:

> " A breaker of his country's laws? Perhaps!
> But there is something that outshines the law
> As certainly as Glittertinde's peaks
> Stand gleaming in the sun above the clouds.
> He was a bad citizen, no doubt;
> For Church and State alike, a sterile tree;
> But up there on the rocky mountain side,
> In the small circle of his hearth and home,
> Where his work lay, *there* I say he was great,
> Because he was himself. 'Twas only there
> The metal he was made of could ring true."

It is then that Peer, with his usual fondness for posing and admiring his own postures, says, having listened to this praise of the dead man: "I might believe that it was myself." And after a little pious philosophizing, goes his way comfortably hugging the picture of himself—"as always—poor but virtuous".

This picture of weakness that accepts its own nature, something that Peer had never really done, made me think once more of Telemachus. For Peer had been trying to be the successful he-man, but always with a false flourish about it, and here also were the very problems of Telemachus, but they were followed up through a lifetime. There was the same sense of weakness, loss of a father and resentment of the power of arrogance in others, but in Peer compensation is continually found in imagination. This is surely, I thought, both his greatest danger and the potential source of his strength. For I had found that the same word "imagination" is

CHAPTER TEN

used in two different senses: in many psychological writings it is used to mean that disastrous recoil from the facts one is not strong enough to control, a turning inwards to the phantasy satisfactions whose logical end is the lunatic asylum; but by Blake it is used to describe the most valuable faculty of man. So also Ibsen makes Peer's imaginings lead him to a trip to the lunatic asylum—but he does not stay there. I thought the reason was that Peer had never allowed his sense of the facts to be completely destroyed, he had, in the first act, refused to pay the price of kingship in the land of the trolls, he had refused to have his eyes tampered with in order to be able to feel that . . . "a sow in short stockings pretending to dance . . . was a beautiful princess . . ." He had refused to be cured of this "troublesome human nature" influencing his vision, the rudimentary capacity to recognize the difference between fact and fancy.

I wondered: 'Is Ibsen saying that the pictures of the mind can only become a strength instead of a danger if personal desire for power has been given up? Is it possible that the difference between Blake's "imagination" and the lunatic's is the difference between the person who has learnt how to make the sacrifice of his desire to be enough unto himself, to be emperor, and the person who has not?'

In my own observations I had been astonished how sometimes the automatic flow of images in my mind were petty distortions of possibility, personal and concerned entirely with making me feel important; while at other times they seemed quite outside the range of personal success or failure, glimpses of simple fact beside which personal achievement seemed quite irrelevant. And I thought that the amount of each kind was definitely connected with the number of times I had remembered to make the inner gesture of poverty. Was it possible that there was only a difference of degree between my everyday struggles to escape from petty personal distortion of fact and Ibsen's problem as a poet in trying to describe universal truths of human nature? I thought his sense of the intensity of the struggle and the difficulty of accepting weakness was particularly shown in Peer's conversations with the Button Moulder:

"PEER GYNT.

But do you mean
That I've got to be melted down
With any Tom and Dick and Harry
And moulded fresh?

No, I say! No! With tooth and nail
I'll fight against it! I'd rather, far,
Put up with anything than that!

BUTTON MOULDER.

But what do you mean by 'anything'?
You must be reasonable, you know;
You're not the sort that goes to Heaven——

PEER GYNT.

I'm humble; I don't aim so high
As that; but I'm not going to lose

A single jot of what's myself.
Let me be sentenced in ancient fashion;
Send me to Him with the Cloven Hoof
For a certain time—say, a hundred years,
If the sentence must be a very severe one.
That's a thing I daresay one might put up with;
The torture would then be only moral,
And perhaps, after all, not so very tremendous.

But the other idea—to be swallowed up
Like a speck in a mass of strange material—
This ladle business—losing all
The attributes that make a Gynt—
That fills my inmost soul with horror!"

There was another theme that interested me very much. Peer, as a middle-aged successful business man, boasts to his admirers that his success is due to the fact that he has never married, he has been enough unto himself. But when he sits, peeling the onion, looking for the kernel of self, he finds nothing. Somewhere I had read "the self is a discovery made in communication", that is, in relation to "an other". But Peer, in trying to be self-sufficient in order to be himself, completely fails to prove to the Button Moulder that he has ever been himself at all. Here surely was the old paradox over again, to save yourself you must lose it, just as that mysterious voice "the Boyg" says "Go round about, Peer".

And what about Solveig? In psycho-analytic terms, I supposed the intrusion of the troll woman to bar Peer's new life with Solveig describes a very common situation; the mother-attracted son who cannot make a happy marriage because the phantasy image of his mother comes between him and his proper love. But was it not also likely that Ibsen would use the idea of Solveig, the ideal feminine-maternal figure, to stand for the creative side of Peer's own nature—since he has already shown in the images used in the song of the threadballs, that he feels the analogy between poetic creation and the bearing of children? And if we love that which we lack in ourselves then by union with Solveig Peer would find the lost part of himself in her. But Ibsen, as a poet, had to find the creating mother principle within himself, not in another, if the threadballs were not to call to him—

> "We are thoughts; you should have thought us,
> We are songs; you should have sung us!"

And to find the Solveig in himself, that could be the mother of thoughts, of true imagination, he had to go back to that other Solveig, as a child to its mother, to utter helplessness—for Peer says on his final return "so speaks a mother to her child".

CHAPTER ELEVEN

In trying to understand the alluring quality of the killing the god theme, I had come across a distinction between two ways in which the mind makes use of mental pictures. Now, in Peer Gynt, I had found the same theme, and in addition, many hints as to the conditions under which the change from one way to the other is accomplished, the change by which imagination becomes the servant of fact rather than a mirage satisfaction of thwarted personal desire. I felt this problem to be of special importance to the weak, since imagination in the second sense is a particular danger for those who feel themselves lacking in sufficient power to force the outer world to give them what they want. It was certainly the problem of Peer Gynt, a ne'er-do-weel and a failure; it was also potentially the problem of Telemachus, thwarted by usurping suitors, although his escape from this into fantasy is not so directly indicated as by Ibsen; but I thought it was hinted at, perhaps, in the picture of Penelope continually weaving and unweaving her web, a fit symbol for imagination that is merely escape. It seemed also to be the problem of Christian, though the sense of weakness is here shown in a more complicated form—a sense of guilt. He surely responds to his own need for utter self-subjection, not by trying to escape from it into illusory dreams of power, but by more direct expression in images of destroying flames and the wrath of God.

But if all these stories were really Odysseys of the weak, what was the real meaning of the end of the struggles? For Telemachus the goal seems to have meant the restoration of his possessions and life at home with his father; for Christian, salvation, immortal life with God in a Golden City. But what did "salvation" mean—being saved, safe? What does it mean to be safe? Slowly I began to wonder whether Peer Gynt did not contain perhaps the clearest hint of what was the true end of all these journeyings and struggles, of what was the real goal and completion of weakness. Was it not really to share and inherit the strength and possessions of the strong, as Telemachus does, and also every woman does who relies on her mate for strength and support? Was it not really to receive a kingdom that is none of one's own making, to sit on golden chairs on either side of a king, as the apostles thought, or to become citizen of some strange perfect city as Christian did ? Was it possible that the only ultimate safety, the only "eternal life", was to be an emptiness that could receive the power of the strong, and with it fashion some new thing—in fact, to be within the mind what a woman is in child-bearing? But perhaps this was what those other story-tellers were actually trying to say in their own way, for this kind of creation is perhaps nothing that one can do with one's own will, it is in a sense riches and a kingdom given to one for nothing, or rather only for the measure of one's emptiness. Was then the "inheritance incorruptible" that

CHAPTER ELEVEN

Christian set out to find really the immortality of the imagination?

Reminded of what Ibsen had said in his introduction to Peer Gynt, I now began to consider what might be the problems of a poet. I thought how the poet is the first explorer beyond the frontiers of accepted knowledge of the human heart; by subtle use of imagery and sound and rhythm, he brings a first order into the wild forest of raw lived experience. To the blind drifted hours in which we simply live without knowing that we live, letting life flow over us in a kind of dream in which fact and illusion are hopelessly mixed, he can give form and name. And by giving this, surely he can give us power to live more effectively, through being aware that we live; and eventually, when the armies of organized knowledge have followed up the pioneer trails of the poets, wisdom can become a public possession; we begin to know something of the facts of our lives and so in part become able to control them, instead of floundering helplessly in the dark. So it was the nameless poets of folklore who invented, for instance, the story of Œdipus, but it required the patient labours of science before the same experience could be put into general concepts instead of particular ones. I began to feel intensely how essential is the part played by the poet in the history of man, how poetry (in the broad sense, including all the arts) is an essential, not a luxury. For man's very existence has depended on his capacity to know the facts. Obviously it was not until he had learnt to know something about the facts of climate and the seasons, of thunder and floods and frost, that he could know how to use these to his own advantage and avoid being destroyed by them. But there were not only external facts he had to know. There were internal facts, facts of his own impulses and conflicting desires, and it was here that the poet was the pioneer. I found myself continually occupied with the thought of how often, through not realizing the nature and strength of their own desires, men have been wrecked by them. One day I read:

> "Because an emotion does not exist or does not become perceptible and active among us, till it has found its expression, in colour or in sound or in form, or in all of these . . . poets and painters and musicians . . . are continually making and unmaking mankind.
>
> "I doubt indeed if the crude circumstance of the world, which seems to create all our emotions, does more than reflect, as in multiplying mirrors, the emotions that have come to solitary men in moments of poetical contemplation; or that love itself would be more than an animal hunger but for the poet and his shadow the priest . . .
>
> "Solitary men in moments of contemplation receive, as I think, the creative impulse . . . and so make and unmake mankind and even the world itself, for does not 'the eye altering alter all'?

> "Our towns are copied fragments from our breast;
> And all men's Babylons strive but to impart
> The grandeurs of his Babylonian heart." [1]

But if man's salvation depended on his capacity to see the facts, both about himself and the outside world, and if the poets were the pioneers in this, what were the

---

[1] W. B. Yeats, 'Essays.'

conditions under which poetry could grow? For a long time I had been puzzled by the continual recurrence of images from the Bible in my thinking. Then I find this note in my diary:

Just supposing this is what the Gospel story is partly about? All this year it's been growing in my mind, the possibility that the Gospel story is concerned, not with morals at all, not with what one OUGHT to do, because someone (God, father) expects it of you, but with practical rules for creative thinking, a handbook for the process of perceiving the facts of one's own experience—and, of course, in this sense, with "salvation", for it is ignorance and blindness which lead to the City of Destruction. And the central truth, is it that only by a repeated giving up of every kind of purpose, plunging into the void, voluntary dying upon the cross, can the human spirit grow, and achieve those progressive fusings of isolated bits of experience which we call wisdom, truth? How it has got so muddled up with morals, I can't quite see—except that symbols created by great minds are immediately seized upon by little ones and used for their own ends—as I suppose I am doing now. For the Gospel story is obviously a Chinese puzzle-box of meanings—I used to think that because I obviously couldn't reach to the inner box it was no good bothering with it at all. But now I know I must use everything, like a caddis worm I must build my house out of everything I can get, I must fight with the angel of the Lord till I force some name out of him, however sacrilegious it seems; life is too difficult to be squeamish. So to me it seems that it is nursery morals which are concerned with "being good" and "being bad", with "ought". I'm sure that the moment you are consciously concerned with being good, priggishness comes in and mental sterility. Real wisdom only grows under the conditions of utter loss of all sense of purpose, standard, ideal, or of being pleased with yourself for being at least partly on the way to your goal. . . .

But what exactly did Jesus say? "I am the Way, the Truth, the Life." Lao Tze also calls his teaching a "way", a method. But how can a person be a way? It must mean "my way". But there are so many people who are always trying to make one believe that their way is the only way. What else did He say?—that the only certain happiness is inside you (that I know quite well but always forget it)—that it grows slowly like a tree from a tiny seed, that it's worth sacrificing everything for, that you must use what you've got, not bury it to keep it safe, that people vary in their capacity for reaching it. . . .

After writing this I came upon a quotation from Blake, again in Yeats's Essays:

"I care not whether a man is good or bad, all I care is whether he is a wise man or a fool. So put off holiness and put on intellect.

"Men are admitted into heaven not because they have curbed and governed their passions, but because they have cultivated their understandings. The fool shall not enter into heaven, be he ever so holy.

"I know of no other Christianity, and of no other gospel, than the liberty, both of body and mind, to exercise the divine art of imagination, the real and eternal world of which this vegetable universe is but a faint shadow, and in which we shall live in our eternal or imaginative bodies when these vegetable mortal bodies are no more. The apostles knew of no other gospel. What are all their spiritual gifts? What is the divine spirit? Is the Holy Ghost any other than an intellectual fountain? What is the harvest of the Gospel and its labours? What is the talent which it is a curse to hide? What are the treasures of heaven which we are to lay up for ourselves? Are they any other than mental studies and performances?

"What is the joy of heaven but improvement in the things of the spirit? What are the pains of Hell but ignorance, idleness, bodily lust, and the devastation of things of the spirit? Answer this for yourselves, and expel from amongst you those who pretend to despise the labours of art and science, which alone are the labours of the gospel.'

But if this were true, how was it that I could also read, in a book by a recognized psycho-analyst:

"Religion, no less than magic, is an expression of the pleasure principle. Like magic again, it belongs to an infantile level of individual psychological growth, and to an elementary stage of social evolution. Religion—or magic —when believed in by men and women or by present-day civilized communities, can only be recognized as a failure to mature—in just the same way as the neurotics and psychotics. In the only kind of complete growing up which is appropriate to the present age, the magical and religious stages should be left behind, as the reality principle takes shape and leads to the interest in objective truth which we call science." [1]

I thought the answer to this apparent contradiction must lie again in the curious Chinese puzzle-box nature of symbols. To say that religion is the same as magic is surely to see only the outside box, to see that religious symbols have been made use of for magical purposes. That religious symbols should be so used seemed to me inevitable. If magic is essentially the result of the childish confusion between thoughts and things, it is

[1] David Forsyth, *Psychology and Religion*, p. 183.

surely natural for the primitive mind to suppose that you can also influence nature in the same way as you influence people, that is, by words and gestures. If you say the right thing to a person he will do what you want; so if you say the right thing to the weather, that is, use the right spell, was it not reasonable to suppose that it also would rain for you when you needed water? And if you were then taught that there were not many spirits controlling what happened to you, not a rain god, a sun god, a war god, and so on, but one God only controlling everything, then it did not make much difference, you still could use your spells, that is, say your prayers properly, and so make sure that everything would be all right.

Looked on as a means for controlling external events, magic from the modern scientific point of view certainly seems childish. But was that the only point of magic? If primitive men were such fools as some modern scientists make out, I often wondered how they ever managed to survive at all. Magic was so universally practised and for so long, was it not probable that it had some useful function, that it was not only a weak-minded and underhand way of satisfying your desire for power? Was it not possible that there was another reason for the practice of magic, that it was used not only because of its imagined effect on the outside world, but because of its real constructive effect on the inner world? If it was admitted that magical practices did serve the useful function of keeping men's hearts up and preventing them from being overwhelmed by terror of the unknown forces against them, was it not also

138

probable that they played a very definite part in the growth of the mind, by giving dramatic expression to internal processes of vital importance? If this were true, then the power of the idea of the crucifixion, for instance, could be due to at least two quite different causes. One, to the survival of magical belief in the power of the blood sacrifice to bring actual safety (or "salvation") to all who sympathetically participated in it, to cause an actual miraculous interference with the course of nature; and the other, to the fact that it was the culminating poetic dramatization of an inner process of immense importance to humanity, a process which was not an escape from reality, but the only condition under which the inner reality could be fully perceived.

CHAPTER TWELVE

THERE seemed to be another reason for the apparent contradiction between the two estimates of religion that I had compared. For I suspected that there was much that passed for "that interest in objective truth which we call science" that was not really so. I remembered a phrase that had caught my attention years before when reading Keats's letters—negative capability. This is how he defines it:

> "*Negative Capability*, that is, when a man is capable of being in uncertainties, mysteries, doubts, without any irritable reaching after fact and reason—Coleridge, for instance, would let go by a fine isolated verisimilitude caught from the Penetralium of mystery from being incapable of remaining content with half-knowledge." [1]

I remembered also how, when I was a student learning physiology, there had been certain passages in the rather simple text-book we were using that left me very confused. Later, when I reached more advanced work, I found that these were all the passages that dealt with places where there was a gap in scientific knowledge of the time. I thought: 'If only the book had frankly said that here our knowledge of the facts was

[1] *Life and Letters of John Keats*, by Lord Houghton.

inadequate, what a lot of worry it would have saved me.'

'To be capable of being in uncertainties, mysteries, doubts, without any irritable reaching after fact and reason,' what did this involve? Certainly it involved a definite emotional relation to the unknown, to the *x* factor; it involved a willingness to face destruction, for the unknown may always contain hidden sources of disaster. I read that to the primitive mind this acceptance of uncertainty is intolerable, both the child and savage thinks he knows; whatever occurs to him as a possible theory he accepts as true, because to him a thought is as good as a fact, it is not a provisional thing to be tested by comparison with the facts. In listening to the man and woman in the street discussing world affairs, particularly the man, I noticed how often he would lay down the law about problems the facts of which he could not possibly know. And I thought that much of so-called science did the same. For real science, the science which Blake coupled with art, must obviously have its face turned equally towards what it does not know and towards what it does, and must also be ready to forego the pleasures that fancied certainty gives.

Somewhere I happened on the remark that religion had done a great service to science in that it taught humility before God and so prepared people for the humility before the facts that science demands.[1] But I wondered, was that service necessarily finished? For if, as I thought, religious practices provided an outlet

[1] Pierre Janet: Unpublished lectures, MS. in British Museum Library.

141

for man's feelings towards the unknown, was it perhaps not a little premature to try and dispense with them? For everyone, whether professedly religious or not, must have some emotional attitude towards the uncertainties of life, whether he call them Chance or Fate or Destiny or God. It may be an attitude of hate and his religion be cynicism, it may be an attitude of fear and his religion be "safety first". In any case, the more unadmitted it is the more it is likely to be crude and childish, since it seems that only those attitudes which are in some way expressed can become truly mature.

This meant, I thought, that in so far as the old forms may be no longer adequate to express our feelings about the universe, many of us are condemned to possess childish religions, unless of course we will bother to find our own forms. For the popular forms, in the West at least, tend to express a belief in the ultimate nature of the universe as good and kind, they personify it as a loving father and mother combined in one, who will supply the good things of life or even grant special treats when asked, to those children who reverence His authority and obey His rules. Many of us in these days, I thought, have felt impelled to reject such a belief simply because it no longer adequately expresses what we feel about the universe. We feel that there is a certain overweening insolence about assuming our right to the position of protected and well-cared for children when the facts about the universe which science is discovering do not seem to give any support to such a belief. Having discovered the mind's power to believe what it wants to believe, we have begun to wonder

whether all the creeds may not be simply "wish fulfil-
ments". So with a sort of grim austerity, some of us
reject all religion, we say that we prefer to face the
truth even though it makes us unhappy, rather than
believe a comfortable lie. And in so doing we feel that
we have made a definite step in the direction of maturity; but, as in all critical moments of growth, does not
this possibility of a step forward also involve the possibility of regression? For we pride ourselves that we
have abandoned one form of expression as childish, but
we have not yet found a better one to take its place. In
fact, in our scorn of what we have just grown out of, we
are inclined to deny not only the value of the expression,
but also the existence of the underlying need which
stimulated it. So the man who heroically repudiates
religion in the name of maturity and truth may go
through life giving intellectual assent to the scientific
view of the universe and still be quite unaware that his
feelings, as distinct from his opinions, lacking the educa-
tive and purging influence of expression, have remained
far more infantile and distorted than those expressed in
the forms he has rejected. As long as he is in a position
where he can make himself believe he is "master of his
situation", as Peer Gynt did, all is well. But as soon as
circumstances, perhaps illness or fatigue even, put him
in a position of weakness, he becomes a sucking baby,
requiring a mother-god to watch over and protect him.
And also his feelings about the universe are as primi-
tively over-simplified as a savage's, full of "good" and
"bad" spirits, gods and devils, good men and enemies
of civilization; often he becomes filled with the most

unreasonable anxieties, even feeling sure he is going to die when he has only got a cold in the head.

I came to the conclusion that many of the anxieties that often clouded my leisure must be of this same kind. But I did not think that the cure for this was to try and force myself back into accepting the tenets of the church; for to do this seemed impossible, it would seem to be going against my most vital impulses, impulses which were apparently less concerned with fixed creeds, than with the everchanging truth of experience. And yet also I did not think I could safely ignore the churches, for they had certainly been the guardians of some of the imagery that I had found most potent.

Of course there were other storehouses of vital images; I remembered, for instance, the bull-fight, and wondered whether I could now understand more why it had seemed to me like a religious ceremony. Was it that it had perhaps organized my feelings, not towards a goodness behind the universe, or an omnipotent power, but towards the facts? Was it for nothing that the Spaniard calls the act of plunging the sword into the bull "the moment of truth?" It is certainly one stage of development, and a necessary one, to have faith in a goodness both within and around you; but it is also necessary to accept a reality, a reality which is also within as well as outside, which is not affected by your ideas of yourself, and to which, sooner or later, in spite of your feeling of power within yourself, you must utterly submit.

I thought the acceptance of the fact of death with full emotional realization, and without fear or self-protection in bitterness or cynicism, is perhaps the final test of acceptance of reality. There were those other ceremonials that had interested me, in which the supreme moment was a killing; but in them the killing was united with the thought of rebirth, it was a sacrifice in order that some good might come, a gift to placate the gods. And I had guessed that if you accept the thought of death with any after-thoughts of immortality it is not a full acceptance. There must be at least one moment of complete blank extinction, a plunge into nothingness. And certainly there was no end to be gained in this killing, the slow defeat of the bull, repeated again and again and again, was sufficient in itself.

I saw of course that the meaning of the bull-fight must have the Chinese puzzle-box quality, meanings within meanings, just as every other ceremonial. So although I have described the tremendous exaltation I felt after the bull-fight, and have tried to express some of the feelings and ideas which it stirred up, I do not suggest that this is what other people must also see in it. I thought that most likely everyone sees in it what he needs to see and that it speaks to each in his own tongue, even to the man for whom the disembowelling of horses overshadows everything else in his memory. As however, no horses were disembowelled the day I went I could not say whether this would have been my language too. Also I could not say whether the exaltation I felt may have been due, not to the ideas I afterwards read into it in my need of some form in which to express my particular problems of the moment, but simply to the effect of sharing intense excitement with a large crowd.[1]

And even if it is not a ceremony in a religion of truth, even if it does not really present symbolically the truth of human life in all its brutishness and defiance and nobility and bewilderment, yet it had given me a form in which these facts could be expressed and so made it more possible for me to face them.

All this would then explain, I thought, why certain religious symbols had so often forced their way into my thinking; it suggested that these might in essence be concerned with the creative spirit of man, with man's capacity to find expression for, and so lay hold upon, the truth of his experience; they might be a history of man's struggle with the angel of God to force his name from him, and all the rest might be secondary exploitation for purposes of personal comfort or social security. Even if they did not have this meaning for others they certainly had it for me, and I was not concerned with argument, but only with finding out where my own mind was leading me by its spontaneous interests. And although it had led me to discover that one wants among other things, pain, suffering, inferiority, it had also led me on to the growing belief that this need to suffer was not in its essence perverse, it was an essential part of the process of perception, it was an impulse to lowness, which if fully accepted, brought richer living and understanding. "As poor yet making many rich" was a phrase that had once haunted me, but I had not

[1] Two years later I saw another bull-fight, in which novices took part, and there was no large crowd, and I hated it.

146

guessed that it was oneself also that would become rich, here and now, flooded with the richness of moment to moment experience. And I remembered also the saying that it were better to enter into the Kingdom lacking an eye or a limb, than having them, to enter into hell fire. Certainly when assertive people made me feel a failure the sense of incompleteness could well be described as like the loss of a limb; and when I accepted the feeling, deliberately accepted loss and emptiness, the peace and richness was just as though I had come into a kingdom. As for hell fire, it well described the torment of anxiety of trying to defend myself against other people's criticism.

As often before, I wondered whether it was not sacrilege to use these historically sacred images for my own mundane purposes. But was there not a story of David who ate the consecrated bread of the Temple when he was hungry? To become self-conscious, to eat of the tree of knowledge of good and evil without also becoming paralysed with shame and the sense of one's own smallness; to develop out of the simple animal enjoyment of the present moment into the capacity to look beyond it, to see ahead and also to remember the past, to be able to do this without becoming weighed down and destroyed by the burden of anxiety, was this "the Way" that Jesus taught? Was this His answer to Adam and Eve's trouble of being shut out of the Garden of Eden? And had not Lao Tze also given the same answer, that you must become the empty vessel if you wished to be filled?

This brought me to a paradox, however: it was in

147

religious traditions that I had found images that seemed to me to be concerned with finding out the truth of the experience of being alive; and yet I had learnt enough history to know that all through the ages it was organized religion that had fiercely set her face against the acceptance of new truths of experience. It was only by a closer study of the nature of images that I came to see how this could be.

CHAPTER THIRTEEN

THE study of feelings having led me to recognize the existence of unexpected impulses, further observations had given me certain ideas about the outcome of such impulses; I now began to consider, not the result of my method, but the method itself.

At the beginning, when trying to recapture childish memories, I had certainly been rather puzzled to find that the straightforward statement of the facts of whatever I remembered, completely destroyed all sense of its importance; also that I could only recapture this sense if I let my mind flow away from the facts to whatever other images occurred to me. Then there had also been that contrast between my passionate interest in wild nature and the more obvious concerns of everyday life; and later when less interested in so-called "nature", I had still found my explorations leading me into paths apparently remote from ordinary life. Why for instance, should I need to see the intimate problems of everyday living and loving and perceiving in terms of witchcraft and pagan ritual? There was another point that puzzled me: I often told myself that many of these questions I was trying to thrash out must surely be fully dealt with somewhere in psychological books, why did I not study those instead of all this vague wandering in mythology? My only answer was that I had not studied these because I could not. I had ranged fairly widely through psychological literature for the purposes of my work, and found it fascinating intellectually, but when I thought of it in relation to my own problems it filled me with despair. I had the same feeling, only more so, about occult literature, I supposed that occultism would have plenty to say about symbols of good and evil, but I could never read such books. There seemed to be an emptiness in all abstractions that reminded me of the masks of devil dancers.

The position then seemed to be that I could neither think about my life in terms of bald fact, nor yet in terms of abstractions. It seemed that the bald fact was too unrelated, it was not any use simply to think about what had happened in terms of he-said and she-said; for that did not get me any nearer understanding the real meaning of what had happened, or make it possible for me to learn from it and so be wiser next time. But neither was it much use to talk about castration complexes and over-compensation and masculine protests as so many of the books did; for though I could recognize the value and truth of such ideas intellectually I could not use them to explain the sense of importance of what I had lived through. They seemed somehow to put out the living glow of experience so that there was nothing there to explain. I did not see at all how they could be a guide for wiser living if in order to live at all one had to forget them. In the hope of coming to understand this more clearly I looked up in my diary an account of a turning point in my life, the time when I was deciding to marry.

CHAPTER THIRTEEN

We had driven about the hills all day, and picked cow-slips. You had said you'd win in the end and that if I would let you kiss me it would be a sign I'd given in—I had been angry that you were so sure you'd win. After tea in that farmhouse we went far out on a rock with the sun going down over the sea and said nothing and you used a little stone to draw mathematical curves on a big stone—then I wanted you to kiss me but was not sure, and then we went back and drove up on to the hill and a thick white sea mist hung over the Downs. We stopped, and we couldn't see anything, only heard cows chumping in the field beside the road. . . . Suddenly we kissed and then drove on in the darkening. You thought it meant "yes" and when I said it didn't I cried, and said how it felt caged if I said yes, and then we drove home.

I had written this, and a good deal more, trying simply to give the facts of this period but with such a sense of the inadequacy of it that I ended with "Oh, I'm so tired of writing all this rot, will it really help me to understand others later?"

Four or five years afterwards when I was amusing myself by trying to draw a sort of pictorial map of my life I found that the picture of this occasion had an important place. I had drawn blindly, not thinking of the meaning of what I did, but now, in my present problem of trying to understand the terms in which my experience expressed itself, I thought I would try to see by writing freely, why I had drawn it as I did.

'. . . there's the setting sun over the sea, that seems quite simple, but what about those two things that look like tombstones?—two stones, the stone he drew curves on, Moses's tables of stone with the law on them—but

151

why those two patterns, they are not what he drew?—
Pythagoras, I remember now, it was on that tombstone
at St. Martha's, when we were children we often wondered who on earth it could be, and the bird-bath
they'd put instead of a marble cross, I used to dream of
him as someone understanding the mysterious laws of
things—there was I think no name on the tomb—and
that pattern on the other stone, it's a harmonograph,
the ones P. used to make in the nursery . . . and I've
kept ever since, mysterious forces making such beautiful
order, as ordered as the pattern on a butterfly's wing—
and that cow, why did I draw that? . . . cows chewing
the cud, placid physical life shut in a field . . .'

At last I saw how the conflict of that moment was
symbolized in the drawing. The cows, which in the
simple description of the facts had been merely pictur-
esque background had become the symbol of a particular view of women's part in marriage, a view that in
those days had often oppressed me. And the mathematical curves scribbled on the stone had been the
symbol of a way of life which seemed to me at that time
totally incompatible with the first; exploration, searching into the mysteries of natural law, the satisfying of
those impulses towards understanding which had led
me first to study 'nature', and later to take up science
and to dream of wandering freely over the face of the
earth.

What should be the way out from the sense of conflict
between these two possible aspects of a woman's life
was a question I could not answer yet. What interested
me at the moment however was the way in which these

spontaneous images at once made clear what had actually been happening, whereas the bare description of the facts had given me no clue.

Although I have called these images spontaneous they did not appear entirely without any effort on my part. I found that I had to keep myself suspended, as it were, over the memory of an experience, to brood over it in a curious expectant stillness, before they would appear. If I did not do this there would simply be the usual vague chatter, my mind would glance at the memory and then slip off on to something else, leaving me none the wiser, but with only perhaps a feeling of regret that it was all over, and a longing to recapture the times that had been happy. But if I deliberately held the memory, with a sort of "brooding on the face of the waters" of the experience, then these images would emerge that had a peculiar feeling of depth and stability, and which banished all longing for the past because they made me feel I still possessed it. There was also another quality about them, they seemed to be deeply rooted in the whole of my body, whereas the casual images that flitted in and out of what Yeats calls the "daily mood" always seemed to belong to the head only. Because of this feeling that they grew out of the whole of me I had called them "organic images", and it was some of these that I had put into the drawing of my life. It seemed to me now that it was only by means of these organic images that I could bridge this gulf between experience as I lived it and abstract knowledge; for while they possessed the glow and reality of lived experience they had none of its isolation, they made it pos-

153

sible for me to link together past and present, and to make the richness of the past available for the present moment. Also they had none of the remoteness of abstract thought, I never had to stop and say, this is all very true and interesting but what has it got to do with me—for in some curious way they were me.

It now occurred to me to wonder whether those primitive rituals which I had found so curiously alluring did not perhaps themselves consist of similar images, expressed in dramatic form. Was it possible that those images which I had called organic were not merely an eccentricity of my own but that always the races of men had known of their power and importance, and so had enshrined them in ritual and myth? I gained further light on this possibility when I came across a particularly self-contained system of images—the art of alchemy. When studying chemistry, I had heard alchemy referred to as an example of man's stupidity, of how hundreds of years of futile activity were spent on the misguided belief that it was possible out of commoner materials to make gold. But now I come across detailed studies of the art, with quotations from writers of the period, stating quite clearly that the real masters of alchemy were not trying to make material gold at all. I found one modern writer [1] concluding from these writings that the raw material of what they call their Great Work is obviously not really lead or fæces or any of the countless other substances mentioned, but human nature, and that the true adepts of alchemy are using chemical symbols to describe a certain mental change.

[1] Silberer: *Problems of Mysticism and its Symbolism.*

What this change actually was, what was the nature of the philosopher's stone, is obviously a difficult question for those who have not undergone the change themselves, but there are many hints that it is a work of creating something. I read:

> "An attentive reader of any alchemical book will not fail to note one important fact—that is, the identity affirmed by adepts to exist invariably between the creation of the cosmos and the operation by which they achieve the Great Work. . . . Whoever has understood the mystery of the creation of the heavens, the earth, the waters, light, the animals, and man knows the secret of the Philosopher's Stone." [1]

This at once made me think of those moments of perception that I had sometimes known when the whole world seemed new created. At one time, I would never have tried to understand these alchemical writers in terms of my own experience, I would have assumed that whatever mystical process these people were talking about was nothing to do with me, since they expressly say it is only the few who can attain it. But now I had learnt that if the imagery fitted I must use it—and I was beginning to find that much of this imagery did fit.

For instance, although a variety of different processes are given as stages of the Great Work, and countless different substances mentioned as raw material, with many and various instructions about the proper type of vessel to be used, I read that the alchemists never ceased repeating: "A single substance, a single vase"; and that

---

[1] *Witchcraft, Magic and Alchemy*, by Grillot de Givry, p. 350.

one adept even said of the traditional operations—"the terms distillation, sublimation, calcination, assation, reverberation, dissolution, descension, and coagulation are no more than one sole and single operation, performed in one and the same vase." Also I read: "The operation of the Great Work is completed with fire, yet here again it is not common fire, which is a brutal and fratricidal fire, destroying instead of creating, but the Fire of the Philosophers, the Fire of the Sages, which does not burn at all, but vivifies."

Also a merchant-goldsmith of Paris in 1756, quoted in the same work, wrote:

> ". . . he who knows how to sublimate the Stone philosophically justly merits the name of Philosopher, since he knows the Fire of the Sages, which is the sole instrument which can effect this sublimation; no philosopher has ever openly revealed this secret fire; he who does not understand it must halt here and pray to God that He may enlighten him."

And in an alchemical drawing of the seventeenth century there is a picture of a man carrying the universe on his shoulders, with a Latin inscription which reads: "Visit the inner parts of the earth; by rectification thou shalt find the occult stone." In the same picture "a triple face on the ground signifies prudence, and a child reading the alphabet indicates that the Philosopher's Stone is a work of infantine simplicity". Finally I read that Nicolas Valois, an alchemist of the fifteenth century, wrote:

> ". . . one grain of the metallic substance can be multiplied to an infinite number so long as the world lasts. For

CHAPTER THIRTEEN

if one grain of the composition of the said Work increases a hundredfold, the second will increase a thousand, the third ten thousand, and the fourth a hundred thousand."

Reading through these passages I was reminded of other images: "infantine simplicity" made me think of—"Whoso does not receive the kingdom of heaven as a little child . . ."; and the multiplying grain of metallic substance was like the grain of mustard seed, or the speck of yeast that leavened the whole.

As by now I was quite used to finding in my mind images from the Bible, I was not surprised at this connection, it only confirmed my suspicion that both those and the alchemical images were referring to a process that was intensely relevant to my everyday problems. I was particularly interested in the phrase—'Fire of the Sages', and in the fact that all the processes of the Great Work were carried on in a special closed receptacle to which great importance was attached. For images of this kind had often come into my mind when trying to describe processes of concentration, long before I had heard anything at all about alchemy. I had felt my thought to be a glowing crucible and the process of becoming concentrated in order to find forms of expression had seemed like a gradual raising of inner fires. Images of fiery vessels held me with a curious power; for instance, I had once found myself haunted all day by the picture of a road-watchman's glowing brazier that I had seen that morning; and once I had woken up with my half-dream thoughts full of the sense of a stone coffin filled with fire, and at once recognized the curious stone boxes called Kist Vaens that I had seen years ago on Dartmoor, and which I was told were obviously coffins, but so small, the body must have been cremated. And another time I had woken up with a vivid sense of the glowing cauldron of the Button Moulder in Peer Gynt. Then of course there had also been that persistent interest in the burning of the god. Remembering this, I now looked up another passage that had struck me in the Adonis chapter of the *Golden Bough*:

"There must have been a special reason for electing to die by fire. The legendary death of Hercules, the historical death of Hamilcar, and the picture of Croesus enthroned in state on the pyre and pouring a libation, all combine to indicate that to be burnt alive was regarded as a solemn sacrifice, nay, more than that, as an apotheosis which raised the victim to the rank of a god. For it is to be remembered that Hamilcar as well as Hercules was worshipped after death. Fire, moreover, was regarded by the ancients as a purgative so powerful that properly applied it could burn away all that was mortal of a man, leaving only the divine and immortal spirit behind. Hence we read of goddesses who essayed to confer immortality on the infant sons of kings by burning them in the fire by night; but their beneficent purpose was always frustrated by the ignorant interposition of the mother or father, who peeping into the room saw the child in the flames and raised a cry of horror, thus disconcerting the goddess at her magic rites. This story is told of Isis in the house of the king of Byblus, of Demeter in the house of the king of Eleusis, and of Thetis in the house of her mortal husband Peleus. In a slightly different way the witch Medea professed to give back to the old their lost youth by boiling them with a hell-broth in her magic cauldron; and

when Pelops had been butchered and served up at a ban-
quet of the gods by his cruel father Tantalus, the divine
beings, touched with pity, plunged his mangled remains
in a kettle, from which after decoction he emerged alive
and young.''

I could not help wondering whether these stories were
not an expression of the same half-seen truth that the
alchemists were talking of under the name of the Fire of
the Sages.

Another alchemical image which interested me particularly was a process called sometimes corruption or
dissolution or blackness. It reminded me now of the
depression and emptiness that so often came upon me
before I could begin to raise the inner fires of concentration. I found in my notes:

> . . . how curious this process of writing is, I must have
> no enthusiasm, no pride in whether I can do it. There
> seems always to be a feeling of futility, that I have nothing
> to say, and usually I try to get away from this by force, by
> looking for something to say, and then my head begins to
> ache; but if I accept this futility, give up my purpose to
> write, and yet don't run away into some other activity,
> just sit still and feel myself to be no good—then the crystal-
> lization begins—after the corruption, blackness, despair.

Certainly my mind seemed to be using these images
in order to think about the process of coming to know
my own experience, and it certainly seemed to prefer
them, as instruments of reflection, to the more usual and
accepted terms of logic and reason. It seemed to prefer
them because they brought meaning and order into the
chaos of raw feeling, whereas conscious reasoning could

159

not touch the chaos, feeling and thought were somehow too much at loggerheads for that. I therefore decided to gather together a wider variety of the organic images I had experienced, and see if I could find out more about how they worked.

CHAPTER FOURTEEN

THE first group of images that forced themselves upon my attention were again those connected with death. When thinking about the death of the god, and the death of bulls, I had come across John Donne's last sermon, preached in London at Whitehall in 1630. I read:

"... After my skin my body shall be destroyed. Though not destroyed by being resolved to ashes in the fire (perchance I shall not be burnt), not destroyed by being washed to slime, in the sea (perchance I shall not be drowned), but destroyed contemptibly, by those whom I breed, and feed, by worms.

"... Miserable riddle, when the same worm must be my mother, and my sister, and myself. Miserable incest, when I must be married to my own mother and sister, beget and bear that worm, which is all that miserable penury, when my mouth shall be filled with dust, and the worm shall feed and feed secretly upon me ... that Monarch, who spread over so many nations alive, must in his dust lie in a corner of that sheet of lead, and there, but so long as that lead will last, and that private and retired man, that thought himself his own forever, and never came forth, must in the dust of his grave be published, and (such are the revolutions of the graves) be mingled with the dust of every highway, and of every dunghill, and swallowed in every puddle and pond. This is the most inglorious and contemptible vilification, the most deadly and peremptory nullification of man, that we can consider . . ."

"Thought himself his own forever," had I not often tried to think that, struggled fiercely against the feeling of being possessed by the being of another? Then I remembered what Keats had said:

"It is a wretched thing to confess, but it is a very fact, that not one word I utter can be taken for granted as an opinion growing out of my identical nature. How can it, when I have no nature? When I am in a room with people, if I am free from speculating on creations of my own brain, then, not myself goes home to myself, but the identity of everyone in the room begins to press upon me so that I am in a very little time annihilated—not only among men: it would be the same in a nursery of children." [1]

And those phrases of Donne's, "mingled with the dust of every highway, and of every dunghill, and swallowed in every puddle and pond", they reminded me of Peer Gynt's terror before the Button Moulder—"to be swallowed up, like a speck in a mass of strange material". How pregnant this image of dust was— "you must mingle your last hour with the dust that marching life has left behind her"—and yet for some it was "the most inglorious and contemptible vilification". But in my own troubles I had often found the idea of being dust the greatest comfort; just as years ago I had loved to imagine myself to be grass, so recently I had used as an incantation in moods of despair:

[1] *Life and Letters of Keats*, by Lord Houghton.

CHAPTER FOURTEEN

"Under a juniper-tree the bones sang, scattered and
   shining
We are glad to be scattered, we did little good to each
   other,
Under a tree in the cool of the day, with the blessing of
   sand,
Forgetting themselves and each other, united
In the quiet of the desert." [1]

Sand was certainly a potent image for me, its echoes
hung about a moment when, somewhere about twelve,
I had lain with my face pressed against the sun-hot sand
of a beach, and felt aware of myself in some new way.
And sometimes now for days together I found myself
repeating—"To be on a level with the dust of the earth,
that is the mysterious virtue".[2]

But if the image of sand held me by its comforting
quality there were other images that held me by the
fascination of horror. I had become aware of them
particularly during the vacancy of mood induced by
strap-hanging in a crowded train of the Underground,
when I would often find my eyes coming back again and
again to a headline or picture in someone else's news-
paper. One day it had occurred to me to consider
what kind of news it was that always so gripped my
attention. But it was easier to intend than to do. At
first I found my mind continually slipping away from
the question, for I had a prejudice against sensationalism and loathed the violent political propaganda of the
kind of newspaper that in fact always caught my attention. Eventually however I brought myself to face the

---

[1] T. S. Eliot: *Ash Wednesday.*   [2] Lao Tze.

163

problem and found that in fact, it was not political news that I ever caught myself staring at, it was odd incidents, such as a picture of whales stranded on the sea-shore, but also, accounts of murders. Yet it was not just any murder, I was never much interested in poisonings or shooting, it was, though I felt it was not at all respectable to admit it, the stories of cut-up bodies that caught my attention with such an entranced horror. It also occurred to me that the only murder trial I had ever bothered to follow right through was the Rouse case; I remembered how the murderer had staged his own mock death by luring a tramp into his car which he had then set fire to, so that the charred body could be assumed by the police to be his own; incidentally it also struck me as rather odd that the only date I remembered in pre-Elizabethan history, apart from 1066, was that of an obscure act called, I think, "De Heretico Conburendo" 1401—that my history mistress had said was very important because it made possible the burning of heretics in the reign of Bloody Mary. As for the "trunk murders", I found myself now thinking about the myth of the dismemberment of Osiris, how that great god who had shown men the use of the plough, given them laws, taught them how to worship the gods, had been trapped in a coffin by his envious brother and finally had his body cut into fourteen pieces.

Thinking over all this, I ventured to re-read what the psychologists had to say, and found that the dismemberment theme was well recognized, and occurred in many fairy-tales; there are apparently frequent stories of a person or animal being cut up and put in a cauldron, or wrapped in a skin or cloth, for the purpose of being brought to life again. This reminded me of Medea's cauldron and Frazer's reference to it when he was discussing purification by fire. But then I read:

"The idea that man himself at procreation or at birth is assembled from separate parts, has found expression not only in the typical widespread sexual theories of children, but in countless stories—and mythical traditions. Of special interest to us is the antique expression . . . which says of a pregnant woman that she has a belly full of bones, which strikingly suggests the feature emphasized in all traditions that the bones of the dismembered person are thrown on a heap, or into a kettle (belly) or wrapped in a cloth."[1]

This seemed to offer an important clue; did it not suggest that the interest in dismembered bodies might be an interest not in death, but in birth? For had I not already been forced to conclude that my interest in death by fire was not only an interest in death? And was not the picture of whales coming up out of the sea also a birth symbol? But if so, I was faced with a question that had cropped up before: was it physical birth or mental birth, was it simply the desire for babies that gave such interest to these things, or was it foreshadowing another kind of birth? Or was it possible that it was both, and that this was another example of the double-sidedness of the meaning of images? Trying to answer these questions I found I had written:

How does all this connect with those other images—the Horned God in the darkness, the Beast, the dark wisdom

[1] Silberer, op. cit.

of the earth, knowledge of herbs that will cure pain, making colours from the natural dyes in plants, the chemistry of natural processes, the pillars of moving sand like the pillar of cloud that led the Israelites—all these things that have allured me?

Have all these symbols, which I seem to have been following after all my life, been simply concerned with the making of babies, the initial surrender of oneself to dark power from the body, which is earth, and the later surrender of one's interests and personal life that the care of a new generation demands? Or have they also reference to another kind of creation, an analogous process, but a psychic, not a physical creation? Perhaps the creation of a new being within oneself—a psychic entity—they said in Fox's day that women had no souls. Is this the struggle to grow one? Perhaps by a process of integration of instincts—a welding process which requires this curious experience that I have called the fire sacrifice and the blood sacrifice—just as heat is required to weld together different chemicals, even to make a clay pot? Or is it that the thing that is born is not a being, but ideas? That the Phoenix that grows out of the ashes is a new idea, a new way of formulating experience, immortal in the sense that it can be handed on from one generation to the next? I don't know but I am certain that something worth while happens, is born out of the blood sacrifice, if only a sense of peace.

But what is the relation of this psychic blood and fire sacrifice to the physical blood and fire sacrifice of sex? I don't know. Was there somehow a confusion of the two in sacred prostitution? But most mystical systems rigidly exclude the physical.

I found that in books on psycho-analysis it was the physical interpretation of imagery that was most considered, symbols of this kind were taken to represent different forms of expression for simple physical desires. But I could not forget Silberer's view that it was of the very essence of symbols that they should have meanings within meanings. The only way to settle the question of which kind of meanings were most important seemed to me to find out which could be used most effectively. If in fact I found I could use what were, in their simplest terms, sexual symbols, if I could use these as instruments with which to reflect about my own experience in general, then I saw no reason why I should not, in fact I might even stultify something by not doing so, I might be throwing away something I could not afford to do without. On the other hand of course I knew it was dangerous to pretend that the physical problems were all solved, the problems of infantile desires, crude fears and possessiveness that Freud had shown beyond any doubt to exist in all of us. But I could not help often wondering whether perhaps these problems of the instinctive life could never be solved completely in their own terms, whether it was only by the understanding of the inner attitudes and movements of the spirit that those outer ones, the simple physical impulses, could ever grow out of childishness.

I now remembered an image that seemed to bear on this problem. It was one of those before-sleeping visions that used occasionally to unfold themselves before me like a coloured moving picture. This time it was a delicate line drawing of a fish against a background of vivid colours; as I lay and watched I had thought vaguely: 'Which way is that fish pointing? it's not upwards or downwards or sideways, not any direction that I know about?' Suddenly I had had a feeling that there was a fourth direction which I called to myself 'inwards' and this, it seemed to me, was the way the fish was pointing.

Of course the sexual symbolism of this was easy to see, but I had the feeling there was more than that. It seemed to me that the fish was disregarding the glowing colours which might stand for the quintessence of all sensory delights, those marvels which in my daily mood I tried to grasp directly—since I never could remember that "he who grasps loses".[1] The fish was disregarding these and pointing beyond them. Was it possible that they were also "all those things" which would be added only if one turned one's face away from them to look for something within?

Was this perhaps why physical sex experience had been ruled out from so many mystical training systems? Was it that the pull of the actual concrete presence and touch of a loved person was so strong that it kept one tied to the concrete, it kept one looking outwards and dependent on circumstances, and so made almost impossible this queer process of letting go the desire for outer stimulus, this willingness to accept death which I had found so fruitful? I had often suspected that the terrific pull of the sexual stimulus was due as much to the symbolism of the act as to physical or biological needs, that sexual experience, for the woman at least, was perhaps the nearest analogy to mystical experience. But this of course would also work the other way, if one

[1] Lao Tze.

CHAPTER FOURTEEN

did not know how to satisfy the physical and biological urge then the symbols of mysticism could be used as a substitute for sex, as they obviously are for instance in some of the mystical writings quoted by William James.[1] This would mean that religious ways of life that prohibit sexual experience would attract those who are anyhow incapable of normal experience owing to some failure to grow through the infantile stages of love.

These thoughts gave me a further idea of the power and hence the danger of these images. They were surely double-faced gods holding dominion over two worlds, one face turned towards the dark regions of blundering animal passion, the other towards the light and clearness of wisdom. This perhaps would account for a contradiction that had often puzzled me, the differing views of the importance of sex. Someone had once said to me: "Why do people make such a fuss! it's such a simple pleasure!" and I thought that in one way this was true. But I also watched my own dreams and images at times when the sexual implication was obvious. For instance:

'I dreamt I had seen a lighted match upon the grass, but had not bothered. Then I found the fire had spread where we had been and a fierce wind had caught it so that it spread to the houses, and I turned back and saw one house after another, six of them, caught up in a mountain of flame and as quickly each reduced to black ashes. And in the ashes I saw there were children, unhurt.'

[1] *Varieties of Religious Experience.*

169

AN EXPERIMENT IN LEISURE

Could I say that the terror and power of those flames stood for a simple pleasure? Then again, I had seen an image which at first I took to be boiling fire in the crater of a volcano, but then had thought it was a spiral nebula, the mass of flaming fire that I had read about when a child, as being the raw material of stars. . . . And once I had tried to see what fire meant to me, and, putting down whatever came into my head, had written:

> Fire . . . rock heaved up from inner fires—fires, fire from heaven, storm and brimstone, destruction, volcanic fire, burning heaths, Moses's burning bush, heat melting the rock, bonfires, the Guy burning, Adonis, that twisted rock at Dunstanborough, twisted by fire, welded, changed, coagulated in the fire, tempered, tempered steel, the blacksmith at Bamburgh, sparks that flew, the clang of the metal, welding and shaping by fire, the burning fiery furnace, Shadrach, Meshach and Abed-nego, living in the fire, living fire, not destructive fire . . .

And then I remembered how a blast like the blast from a white-hot furnace had once enveloped me in the middle of a crowded city:

> May 11. Magdalen Tower flood lit, shining out against the dark buildings with a still supernatural glow. I suddenly felt the proportion of the tower to the body and it shattered my world of time. I've felt that before, delightedly, about some picture—time stood still or something crystallized beyond it—but here it was not a sudden suspended peace that had come upon me, but a challenge, a terrifying power that could blast all familiar things. I once heard a story that for every man there was a certain

170

chord of notes that was the same as the harmony on which his body was built, and, if it was sounded loud enough, it would destroy him in an instant. So the proportion of that tower has power to destroy my world utterly. I felt a sudden impulse to fall forward under a passing bus in order that I need never have the image clouded, die on the crest of it before the transfiguration became blurred.

I knew that church towers were commonly looked upon by psycho-analysts as a sexual symbol, so I wondered again whether this was a disguised imaginary satisfaction of physical desire, or whether it could be a symbol of something else. For lack of further knowledge I could only again assume that it was both, for I remembered, "never is the external truly real"; it is only effective when "fortified by thought".[1] So I began to see these images that held me with such power and had such a quality of being "truly real" as striding the gulf between the inner and the outer, between crude physical facts of bodily life and the truths of the growth of mind.

About this time I happened to re-read what Jung had said about images, a passage [2] which I had often read before, but without any comprehension of its significance for me—I read:

"The image is a concentrated expression of the total psychic situation . . . The image is equally an expression of the unconscious as of the conscious situation of the moment. The interpretation of its meaning, therefore, can proceed exclusively neither from the unconscious nor

[1] Groddeck: *Exploring the Unconscious.*
[2] Jung: *Psychological Types.*

AN EXPERIMENT IN LEISURE

from the conscious, but only from their reciprocal relation."

If Jung were right, then no wonder that I had found that the study of images was the surest way to find out what I wanted.

CHAPTER FIFTEEN

HAVING found out to some extent what some of my impulses seemed to be concerned with, I now tried to see these impulses in a wider context. Several times, during the course of this experiment, I had tried to re-state what I was doing in as many different terms as possible, so that I should not so easily slip into forgetting it, slip into all the mistakes and depressions that I had found came with blind living. Several years before, I had made a note:

> ... revolt against nature, it's so unformed—in the small, yes, there's form there, in the shape of flowers, cells under the microscope, the pattern on a butterfly's wing, crystals, living bodies—but it's so inchoate in the large. Just roaming the country is not now what I want, I want form, crystallization, that timelessness of fine paintings ... I don't want to wander abroad seeing things, I want quiet and a rhythm of routine, so that I can bring form out of this chaos of nature, raise the fire within till something crystallizes into shape ... "I'll go no more a-roaming" ...

This idea of crystallization had developed through the months till I had become full of this thought of shaping one's life into a whole, in order somehow to possess it:

> June 15. . . . Organizing one's life in the present, bringing all activities and desires into relation with one

another, but also into relation with the past, giving it depth, another dimension. And these things that come up out of the past, a sudden memory as I look now at the passing country out of the carriage window, at these Thames water meadows, memory of finding arrowhead growing in the Pevensey dykes, the intense emotional warmth of the discovery—and of skullcap and purple loosestrife that first time I saw the Thames—how I tried to possess them, picked them, photographed them, drew them, sometimes dug them up and tried to make them grow in my own garden—but they slipped away, eluded me, after the first intimate shock of discovery—those pink butterfly shells at Bamburgh and then—those herbs that I tried to grow in my garden—and vegetable dyes, finding dyer's greenweed and boiling strips of alder bark— somehow with the essence of their colour I possessed them more—that wild drake we saw over the dark woods and I drew a picture of him—how it filled the whole day with intense importance—and those dark schemes of child- hood, Falmouth, the warm air and dreaming of making a lasso, longing for a black doll, planning a strawberry bed, making that embroidered waistcoat and the clay lamp— all these memories lie in my body, not in my head— looking out from this train at that June chalk bank—the blue milkwort and trefoil and grass—it gets deep inside me, under my skin, into the marrow of me, as if I was actually made of it—but didn't Blake say: "Out of every plant and beast man's self cries to him"?—I thought at first that meant a poetic way of stating the fact of evolu- tion, but now it seems to be true in a more intimate way, that these loves are the images which your dim sense of what you are takes to clothe itself, they become the very texture of your sense of being.

I remembered now the first moment when such an

idea had dawned upon me in a dim way. Once, when I was nineteen or twenty, I had written:

> August 8, Sussex. . . . It has been a day of harvest, men ceaselessly loading the blue wains from sunrise to sunset. Now the stubble fields lie bare and glowing in the twilight. . . .

I had stopped writing because the rest of my feeling had seemed a poetic affectation. But I still remembered what at the time I would not admit—the spreading fields had seemed to burn with more than the light of sunset, as if the glowing fires of earth had been laid bare by the cutting of the corn: in those miles of flat rich cornland under the still sky, I had felt the earth as a living thing —and for an instant, had felt as though my own body were the earth.

Then I went on with my speculations about interest in nature:

' . . . to follow up passions, then, every little passion for a flower or a shell or a wild duck, is it collecting all your scattered self? And sometimes you find it in people—I remember that love which began with the thick almond buds of February, and seemed to share with them the feeling of rich possibilities slowly unfolding—but when my love went away, in July how I hated the heavy summer green of trees, hated their rich brooding apart over something that I felt now shut out from.'

One day I thought:

' . . . is it possible that to know the truth of the experience of being alive perhaps the whole universe is necessary to provide pictures for one's understanding?'

Was this why parts of physical geography had so intimately gripped my imagination, fires in the earth, trade winds bringing rain, cyclones, deep ocean currents and the magnetic force of the Pole? Otherwise, what had these to do with me, I was never going to pilot a ship, or make plans to irrigate a country. But as pictures of the mysterious motions and seasons leading to the fertility of the body and the mind, they were most intimately my concern.

' . . . if each of these interests, these sudden feelings of immense importance—a Moorish look to a horse's collar, a cliff over the Hudson River—if each of these is the first intimation of something I am going to find in myself, in my own personal experience, in day to day living with others, then I am sure I must not stop at mystery or mysticism, it is everyday human experience that comes first and last and all the time. The rest is only a help to understanding it, instruments of reflection.

'I've so often wondered what "spiritual" meant—something remote that I could never attain to? But we use the word often—"a man of spirit", "her spirits rose", "rest to the spirit", "a spirited performance", "the spirit of a place, a nation, a man's work". So, spiritual things are not remote things, but vital things—like Catherine of *Wuthering Heights* I think I'd cry for earth if I ever found myself in heaven.

'Is this why the goal of the Odyssey is more intimate and real to me than the goal of *Pilgrim's Progress*? To be trying to get home to one's own place—the love in that phrase "sea-girt Ithaca"—wife and child rather than a glowing city of gold. Of course, it does emphasize the fact that in a sense you must, like Christian, leave wife and child in order to find them, you must be willing to live your life alone—for Odysseus had already done that.'

I now thought I understood a little better all those early interests whose power had so puzzled me. Those years of preoccupation with the mating of birds, with nests and migration and the season for each bird's singing, I could now say two things about it; I could say that it seemed to be premonition of the facts of physical sex life and of maternity that lent the gleam to these things; but I could also say that the living processes I needed to understand were not exclusively physical, and that the mind used the idea of the physical facts of sex and maternity themselves as symbols, symbols of the truth that all real living must involve a relationship, recurrent moments of surrender to the 'not-self'. Richness from the earth, whether the healing power in herbs, bright colours hidden in the chemistry of leaves and roots, or the dark wealth of mines, all these were equally apt ways of talking about either the powers of generation in the body, or the unknown creative depths of mind. A sudden voice in the dark, fireflies, birds whose ways and songs were strange to me, all these had been heralds of experiences beyond the bounds of anything I knew; and those dead rivers of Arizona, shallow rivers, polluted rivers, these, I thought, were signs enough that the need to break the barriers of my known experience had been imperative. Actually, while first feeling the pull of these images, I had known that my greatest conscious desire was to bear a child; but the fact that when I had fulfilled this desire the images still held me seemed to be proof of their double meaning. Meteor City, that we never saw, riches fallen from the skies—certainly all the joys of being alive felt like this, as well as the astonishing fact of a new human being emerging from one's own body.

And then the actual people I had loved, the idea that what I saw in them was also in a sense a symbol, explained many things. Before I had begun this search I used to feel sad when I thought of loves that had passed, as if I had lost something, and I felt a fool for having thought someone was a god. But now I thought it was not really loss, each had given me something, they had given me a clearer picture of what it means to be alive, and I need not throw it away because I could see now it was not the whole picture, or the only picture. Memories of an adolescent companionship, beginning at eleven or twelve, now seemed to hold the essence of the matter:

'. . . that day we went with crabbing irons to far-out rocks that the low spring tide had just uncovered, we'd never seen them before—and in the pools we found curious sea creatures, a new world of colours and shapes —unguessed-at ways of living.'

So with each love had come new glimpses of experience. At twenty, when I had once persistently refused to let a new friendship develop, because I was afraid of its power, I had dreamt:

CHAPTER FIFTEEN

'. . . I was in the bedroom of some house, there were lace curtains over the window, outside I heard music, I looked out and there were gipsies passing, going away to practise their music on the heather far away to the north. I ached to go with them, but could not, was impeded by heavy luggage and other things.'

This dream had made a great impression on me, I had decided I must be letting my fears stifle the growth of experience, I was shutting myself away from the gipsy music on the heath, simply because I was not ready to face the power of it.

The mysterious force by which one is lived, the "not-self", which was yet also in me, it was this force that I must learn to know, and to remember continually without fear, a force which had seemed sometimes like a beast within, sometimes like a god. And if to find a continual conscious relation to the source of life inside you, the thing that lives you, that possesses you, if that was what all my wanderings had been aiming at, it was no wonder that the theme of physical sexuality had also been involved. Also no wonder the question of whether this thing inside you was something to be trusted had become a burning one; for at first I had only known it as the force of desire, unreasonable emotion sweeping me against my will, like a small bird in a gale, sweeping me into panics of shyness, obstinate silences, bursts of rage or hate—and certainly these were not anything to be trusted. But I could see now how gradually there had grown an awareness of another aspect of it, gradually I had become aware that there was something else in me, something that knew as well as felt, something more than gusty wayward impulse. Ten years before, I had written in my diary, under the heading of "The Uncertainties"—

Is there any wisdom other than our reasoning, expedient, conscious minds?

Now I could answer that I was certain there was, if you chose to look for it. Whether it was there all the time, or whether in some curious way, one's looking for it made it, I could not tell.

While thinking of all this, I remembered that I had one day made some "free drawings", just as I had sometimes done "free writing", quite without thought of their meaning; now it occurred to me that they perhaps showed the stages of finding that the force by which one is lived is something that can be trusted. The method of drawing had been quite simple. I had provided myself with a pile of rough paper, filled my brush with whatever colour seemed most attractive at the moment, and then begun idly to spread the colour over the paper. I had had no preconceived plan, but had let my brush follow any shape that was suggested by the first dab of paint, and in this way had covered six sheets in the course of half an hour. Definite ideas had sprung up from each while I was painting it, but I had hardly noticed these at the time. Now however I thought I would try to develop them by writing them down.

(1) . . . the head of a sheep, silly looking, pink, rather a silly colour, silly pink bows.

(2) . . . a dragon dancing a jig, but she's got a skirt on and hob-nailed boots, like a charwoman who is a little drunk—and the sun is rising over the desert, it's the same dragon I drew when I was fifteen, but she's not terrifying now, even a little absurd.

(3) . . . a wolf in the dark.

(4) . . . she looks as if she is meditating, and what an un-comfortable position—and it's blue, that particularly soulful colour.

(5) . . . this is a queer one, the cauldron has got those hob-nailed boots again and a leering grin—that spike on it makes me think of the water scorpions we used to find in streams and those curious egg-laying spikes that female grasshoppers have—as for the snake, I feel respectful towards it, it's not destructive or loathsome, I feel somehow it's a beautiful thing, wasn't there some snake in the Bible that was good, not evil? Oh yes, surely Moses held up one for the sick people to look at and they were healed.

(6) . . . the door of a temple, inside it's glowing with supernatural fire, it's a climax of a ceremony, the de-scent of white hot fire from heaven—but it also makes me think of Shadrach, Meshach and Abed-nego, who were cast bound into the burning fiery furnace and were not burned, but were seen walking freely—and a fourth with them that Nebuchadnezzar said was like the Son of God.

To me it seemed that the first two of these, the silly sheep associated with pink bows, and the crudely dancing dragon that was also a charwoman, both these represented aspects of the feminine side of desires. For the sheep reminded me of a dream I had once had:

'. . . a horned god, I knew it was Dionysus, was

towering over me, almost enveloping me, for I was wedged in a cleft between two great stones and could not move—I heard his voice commanding "You must say 'yes', you must say 'yes'!" and the "yes" sounded like the bleat of a sheep. I did not answer for I felt that once I had said "yes" I would be lost—instead I tried to bite him . . . but finally I gave in.'

Thinking over this I remembered the cow in one of my other drawings and the placid life of fenced-in dependence it had stood for. I also thought how all my life I had been aware of the impulse to agree with people, never to stand alone, and how ashamed I had been of this, I had struggled against being a sheep. As for the dragon dancing a jig, I knew that the dragon was a symbol with layer upon layer of meanings. For me it had once stood for death, for loss of the sense of self, it was a terrifying and loathly creature; and in this sense it had also seemed to stand partly for physical desire, and the loss of awareness of the ego that came with physical sex experience. But this dragon was not like that, it was not a terrifying thing, it seemed to me to be a happy dragon, dancing before the rising sun—although a little crude in its hob-nailed boots. Did the picture perhaps record the fact that I had now learnt to look on physical sex experience, neither as terrifying annihilation, nor yet as the highest peak of existence and the only gateway of salvation—however much it might feel like this at passionate moments?

But there was clearly another aspect to this force by which I had been lived, besides being swept away into sheep-like agreement and dependence, and into the enjoyment of bodily sensation, there was also the dark destroying power of the third picture, the "big bad wolf". This surely was the complement of the other two, it was the primitive impulse to power which matched the primitive impulse to submission, it was the awareness of one's capacity to destroy, the dark stirrings of violence that surged up when I was angry, dark because it very rarely reached the surface. And then the sitting figure in blue, this made me think of my impulse to dream, sometimes so strong that I could not tell at all what was going on around me. In this drawing I was suspicious of the glow being confined to the head only, and of the slouching position, there seemed to be something unbalanced about it, something mock ethereal. In fact, it seemed an apt symbol of that other kind of turning inwards, the turning inwards blindly, which is actually a retreat from the reality of fact rather than a way of reaching it. Clearly it was the confusion between these two ways of turning inwards, the blind grasping after dream pleasures, and the seeing willingness to let all pleasures go and simply wait, it was this confusion which was the greatest danger of the contemplative life. This thought also reminded me of the parrot's feathers in my fairy tale, that the fishes found so useless in their efforts to light the black depths and bring to life the skeleton playmate. For I had certainly spent much of my life in fruitless running after the coloured parrot's feathers of fancy, fruitless because it was blind, it was imagination still in the service of desire rather than of fact.

I thought there was nothing ethereal about the next

183

picture. The leer on the cauldron reminded me that I had read of this thing called the ID that it is greedy, malicious, longs to have its rights; and the shape of it made me think of what I had also read:

> ". . . it often does not know whether it is a man or a woman, for in the being we call a man there lives also a woman, in the woman too a man . . ." [1]

And again, as in the dragon picture, there were the hobnailed boots, crude, clumsy life. But what of the snake? It seemed to me that something was growing out of the fire of passion, a new power; I wondered if this could perhaps be foreshadowing a possible change in the force by which one was lived.

And then the last picture, the many figures united in a single purpose of concentrated waiting, united in the enclosed fiery space. Was this perhaps a premonition of the fire that could weld the wayward impulses to violence and lustfulness and pleasure-seeking dreams into a new thing, so that the fiery furnace of the mind, when concentrated and still, could become possessed by another presence, something other than either blind impulse or deliberate and laborious reasoning, a free spirit for whom the ego which one calls one's self is entirely irrelevant?

Such images as these certainly gave form to feelings of compelling power that had grown during the course of this experiment. Just in so far as I held myself still and watched the flickering movements of the mind, trying to give them expression in words or drawings, just

[1] Groddeck.

so far would I become aware of some answering activity, an activity that I can only describe as a knowing, yet a knowing that was nothing to do with me; it was a knowing that could see forwards and backwards and in a flash give form to the confusions of everyday living and to the chaos of sensation. I still felt I was being lived by something not myself, but now it seemed like something I could trust, something that knew better than I did where I was going. Once I had bothered over whether you should have a purpose in life or just drift along; now I was sure that I must do neither, but, patiently and watchfully, let purposes have me, watch myself being lived by something that is "other".

Reviewing these conclusions, I could not help comparing them with the beliefs of a certain religious revivalist movement which was just then growing in popularity. I had once attended one of their meetings, and had all the time felt that these people were really play-acting; although they obviously thought themselves to be intensely serious and they talked a great deal about sincerity, I felt that they were continually burlesquing certain fundamental truths, I had the same vague uneasiness that one sometimes gets at seeing a clever but cruel parody of something that one knows to be of fundamental importance. More than this I could not say at the time, but now I tried to state explicitly what I felt about this meeting.

Certainly I had found that there was something—not one's self, in the ordinary sense of the word "self"—that could be a guiding force in one's life; but I thought it would be insolent to call this God. Also I remembered the main paradox of my discoveries, the fact that the price of being able to find this "other" as a living wisdom within myself, had been that I must want nothing from it, I must turn to it with complete acceptance of what is, expecting nothing, wanting to change nothing; and it was only then that I had received those illuminating flashes which had been most important in shaping my life. But the "Buchmanites" seemed to me to be completely dominated by their desire to change things, particularly to "change" people.

I found the implications of this paradox sufficiently bewildering however; for surely many of the people who had done most for mankind in adding to the richness of life were people who had, in fact, set out with a burning desire to change things? Ought I not to pay for my inheritance by also "doing my bit" in the way of trying to change things, trying to make life better for everybody? Or was it perhaps that there were just certain temperaments for whom the desire to change things was fatal to fruitfulness. I could not tell, I could only state what seemed to be the truth of my own experience, the observation that if I did my job with any uplifting enthusiasm for "doing good" what I did was badly done.

And there were other points of divergence that became clear to me now. I had found that not only must I have no purpose, I must expect nothing, but also any clinging to the remembrance of past experience interfered with the renewal of it. I found that even giving the name of "the fire-sacrifice" to something, had made me expect that something to be the same as it had been, and so had prevented me seeing the ever-new present. But the "Buchmanites", by their use of a jargon to describe what they expected to happen to people must surely dam up the flow of experience. Was this why I had felt so many of the people who spoke at the meeting were repeating empty words? And yet, paradox again, I had continually found that I must try and give names to my experience, it was only by trying to find words for it that it seemed to grow; but when I found words, I must let them go again, never cling to them or they would become a dead thing. I had suspected often before, and this confirmed my suspicion, that for me at least, there was no method for salvation, richness came only when I faced experience naked of expectancy or hope—"the readiness is all".

It seemed then, that all these years I had apparently been trying to reach after, grasp, comprehend, this mysterious and astonishing fact of simply being alive. I knew to many people this would seem a futile preoccupation, and in many moods it seemed so to me too; I remembered again a scornful reference I had read in some American book review to the fact that there are actually some people in the world "who are more interested in experience than in getting things done". And yet it was not I who had chosen this preoccupation, I had actually blinded myself to its existence for twenty or thirty years and had gone my ways assuming that it was my business in life to get things done. But now, deeper than all my practical ambitions and belief in action, was the guess that Yeats was right, that in fact the forms in which man expresses his sense of being alive are as powerful a force for change, though in a different way, as any deliberate attempt to get things done, because it is these which change men's hearts—particularly one's own heart.

CHAPTER SIXTEEN

BEFORE I began this experiment I had always been haunted by the feeling that the surface of life, what everyone said about it, was quite different from the reality of life, that the important things that were happening all the time were on the whole quite different from what was said about them. This had often made me feel the impossibility of real communication; when I tried to tell anyone about something that had happened I was made dumb by the contrast between the poverty of words and the reality of living. For years this contrast had oppressed me to the verge of hopelessness, for I had often moved in circles where every person was judged by what they said—and quite rightly, too, I thought, for of what interest to others was an experience that could not be communicated—also had I not myself continually found that it was only through expression that there was mental growth? And yet knowing this, I still could not tell people what I had found interesting, I had to be content with conventional phrases and know that what was really important must remain unsaid. But I thought that this preoccupation with the unexpressed whole of what happened was a subtle poison, I often found myself saying, "For he on honeydew hath fed, and drunk the milk of paradise"—it was a mirage joy that unfitted one for the business of living.

AN EXPERIMENT IN LEISURE

Time and again I would find that I shirked the effort
to speak of something because the effort seemed to kill
the reality of the experience; especially was this true in
drawing. I would settle down with my paper, full of
enthusiasm and inspiration, only to find that after the
first few lines the whole idea had faded, there was
nothing but a bored blankness in my mind, and an
utter inability to know where to put the next line.

For years I had continually thus felt myself suspended
in the blankness between expression and the inner
vision of the facts. But now I had learnt that I must
accept the blankness, since it was from this that an
image would grow, an image which was communicable
because it was a picture of some *thing*, of flames or dust,
or a horned beast; but which also somehow contained
within itself the inner truth that I had found utterly
incommunicable in terms of matter-of-fact statement.

The discovery of the power of these images had certainly been a great surprise to me. I had once heard it
expressly stated that experiment showed images to be
useless in thinking, a mere vestige of more primitive
forms of thought that actually disappear altogether
amongst expert thinkers; and I had assumed it was my
job to try and make my thinking more expert. But
now I was finally forced to admit a fact that had long
been staring me in the face, the fact that deliberate
efforts to think out the problems of my life were always
failures, if by "thinking out" one meant deliberate step
by step reasoning. Instead, I was finding that it was
the despised images that made a sensible and ordered
life possible, not reasoning at all. Was this a sign of

primitive mentality? If so, it was high time I faced the fact and made the best of its primitiveness, rather than trying to make show of using a logical intelligence which I did not possess.

It was in relation to moods that I experienced the power of images most particularly. I had long since discovered that control of moods was one of the dominant problems of my life, that time and again I could work out what was the reasonable thing to do or say, but because of my mood I could not do it. At one time I had thought that moods could be controlled by an internal gesture of acceptance, of relaxation, of surrender; now it seemed that this internal gesture was only half the picture, from it emerged an image, and it was the image that seemed to be the pivot of the mood. I was liable for instance, to wake up in the morning feeling depressed and resentful because I could not have what I wanted in some matter. Of course I would tell myself countless times that this was real life and the only sensible thing to do was to accept it, since there were millions of people with infinitely worse troubles. But such reasonableness would have no effect whatever on my mood. Then, like a sudden emergence into fresh air, an image would fill my mind; and after it I would feel that my infantile desires to have all the pleasures in the world had not just been shouted down by reason, they had been welded into a deep peace. Sometimes it was the picture of Apollyon that occurred to me, especially when the morning depression hung round the thought of all the things I must do if I was to have what I wanted, a heavy burden of plans and busyness. I could interpret Apollyon as an image of my reliance on my own will, the feeling that it was myself that did things, as against all my experience that it was only when I forgot all idea of myself that my actions were really fruitful; but it was the image that had power over my wilful mood, not the mere verbal statement of what my experience had taught me.

Of course, there were not only peace-giving images that could turn moods from worry to calm, but also storm-giving ones. Once, in the middle of happy chatter with two other people, I had suddenly found myself plunged into gloomy hatred of them both. Afterwards tracing back what had been in my mind, I realized how something had been said that had brought back a vivid image from childhood of some situation in which I had been made to feel insulted and cast out. Of course I knew storm-giving images, and others of their kind that brought sudden panics and confusions, were the special province of the psycho-analyst, but as far as I could see psycho-analysis proper had limited its studies to this kind of image, it had not concerned itself very much with the other kind, that I can only call the peace-giving images, which seemed to be no less powerful.

Now also I could see that during all those years of being haunted by a bottomless gulf between expression and the facts as I felt them, I had thought of expression as a clear-headed logical statement, as it appeared to be for so many other people I knew. So many of them seemed to live all their days in the world of expression, what was said was all that existed for them, they never seemed to let their glance slip beyond the words, to grow bewitched by the boundless spectacle of the facts as one simply lived them. In this I envied them, for the boundlessness of this spectacle could be also horrible, terrifying. I envied them their calm certainty about life, the ease with which they settled every doubt with a quick word. Often I remembered a conversation I had once read:

"One entered the world, Denis pursued, having ready-made ideas about everything. One had a philosophy and tried to make life fit into it. One should have lived first and then made one's philosophy to fit life . . . Life, facts, things, were horribly complicated; ideas, even the most difficult of them, deceptively simple. In the world of ideas everything was clear; in life all was obscure, embroiled. Was it surprising that one was miserable, horribly unhappy? Denis came to a halt in front of the bench, and as he asked this last question he stretched out his arms and stood for an instant in an attitude of crucifixion, then let them fall again to his sides.

" 'My poor Denis!' Anne was touched. He was really too pathetic as he stood there in front of her in his white flannel trousers. 'But does one suffer about these things? It seems very extraordinary.' . . . 'Why can't you just take things for granted and as they come?' she asked. 'It's so much simpler.'

" 'Of course it is,' said Denis. 'But it's a lesson to be learnt gradually.' . . .

" 'I've always taken things as they come,' said Anne. 'It seems so obvious. One enjoys the pleasant things, avoids the nasty ones. There's nothing more to be said.' " [1]

[1] *Chrome Yellow*, by Aldous Huxley.

AN EXPERIMENT IN LEISURE

The Denis of the story had certainly also seen the spectacle of the unexpressed, seen it as "obscure, embroiled, horribly complicated"; and for him also expression had apparently meant "ideas", a world in which everything was clear, a world which one argued about logically. I wondered whether the way out for him, as for me, would have been to seek after, not ideas and logical argument, but images, those two-faced gods who bridge the gulf between what is spoken and what is felt, between the seen and the unseen, between spirit and flesh, bridge it because they are an outward and visible sign of an inner and private experience. And the impulse to suffer, that the Anne of the story found so extraordinary, was not this the same impulse that I had discovered, the impulse which at first glance was just a tendency to self-laceration, but which if accepted and understood could lead to a freeing of the imagination from the dominance of the ego.

It seemed to me now that the main part of my enterprise could be described in terms of the difference of temperament between the Annes and the Denises of the world. The differences between those whose interest is for some reason biassed towards what is visible and expressed, and those who are biassed towards an inner mental life, these differences seemed to me now to be fundamental in every activity. If you have once turned inwards and become aware of anything more complicated than the comforts and discomforts of digestion and appetite and sensory pleasures, then you are at the mercy of terrors that seem far to outmatch the dangers of the external world, you are at the mercy of past and future, you can become obsessed by memories and forebodings, "the dark backward and abyss of time", can become a looming presence overshadowing and threatening your own existence. It can make you feel you are as nothing, nothing to say, nothing to feel, nothing to be—and to defend yourself against this you may plunge into wild assertiveness, laying down the law, as the shy person who talks too much to cover his shyness; or it may make you completely tongue-tied and unable to do anything. And whatever you do, you bungle it, for your attention is not there to attend to ordinary things, it is held by the Medusa vision of disaster. But the way out of this, I was sure, was not to try and copy the Annes—that was really impossible, for what you have once seen you cannot unsee—but there was another way, the way of the Chinese sage who said: "Empty yourself of everything and remain where you are." Was not the very obsession with disaster and failure simply due to your spirit, unknown to you, driving you on to this acceptance of emptiness?

Once a man of about thirty had said to me: "Oh, but Lao Tze's is an old man's philosophy, it is a retreat from life". So might a pupil in jiu-jitsu object that it was cowardice to wait and let his opponent spend his strength upon him. So Lao Tze also says: "By non-action there is nothing which cannot be effected". I had come to believe that, short of being a retreat from life, this wiping out of oneself was the only way by which certain temperaments, at least, could come to act effectively at all.

Before this time I had often tried to read Jung's

Psychological Types, but found much of it impossible to understand, as so often with books that too deeply concern oneself. Now I opened the book at random and found that Jung had said of the person who is more dominated by the inner-life than the outer:

> ". . . as against our occidental world-philosophy, he finds himself in the minority, not of course, numerically but from the evidence of his own feeling. In so far as he is a convinced participator in the general style, he undermines his own foundations, since the present style, with its almost exclusive acknowledgment of the visible and tangible, is opposed to his principle. Because of its invisibility he is obliged to depreciate the subjective factor, and to force himself to join in the extraverted over-valuation of the object. He himself sets the subjective factor at too low a value and his feelings of inferiority are a chastisement for this sin."

Before, I had never been able to understand what the phrase "subjective factor" might mean. Now I could see that under many names my mind had been driving me to recognize it throughout the whole of this experiment. Whether I had called it the *x*, the unknown factor, the force by which one is lived, whatever I had called it there seemed to be only one conclusion about it—that I must learn to trust it completely. All my experience had taught me that this was the only way to prevent the sense of blankness that would otherwise catch me unawares and sweep me to despair. With this in mind I now made a rule and found it worked, though not always: that whenever I was aware of the ability to choose what I would think about (and this was only at recurrent intervals during the day, in between whiles I thought blindly, without awareness) then I must stop all effort to think, and say: "I leave it to you". I must let go all thinking that I knew, and the sense of power that knowing something gives, and accept blankness.

I realized now that the intensity of the struggle against this sense of blankness had affected all my relations with other people. Once, in recent years, I had had an angry quarrel with the person I was nearest to; when I heard the front door shut as he abruptly left the house I was filled with an impotent rage that seemed utterly beyond words; acting on a sudden impulse, I ran to get paper and pencil and began wild scribbling. At first what I was drawing seemed to be a snake around a tree-trunk, and I was still angry and hopeless—but I went on elaborating the lines, just as fancy took me. Eventually I produced the drawing shown in Fig. 3 and found that by now my anger had entirely evaporated into amusement at what I had produced; at first I thought it was a sort of female Punch, and then suddenly saw that it was also the Duchess in *Alice in Wonderland* who always screamed "Off with her head". At once this gave me a clue to the reason for my impotent and boundless rage, for I remembered all the people from my childhood upwards, mostly women, since I had been educated by women, who by sheer force of a loud voice or a show of anger or sarcasm, had had the power to make me "lose my head", to wipe out from me all sense of my own identity, not only to thwart me in what I wanted, but to produce such a state that

197

AN EXPERIMENT IN LEISURE

I no longer knew what I wanted at all, I was aware only of them, utterly possessed by them. In a lesser degree I had known of the same thing happening, not only when someone was angry with me but whenever I was in contact with the kind of person who was sure

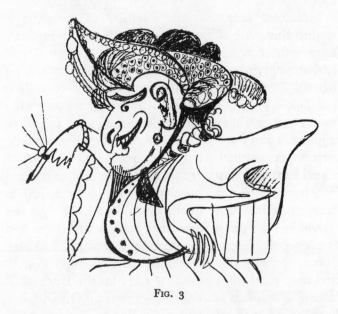

Fig. 3

about everything, my automatic response seemed to be sure about nothing, not even who or what I was, my mind ran round in futile circles, like a rabbit chased by a stoat.

Remembering how Keats had described himself as feeling the identity of everyone in a room pressing upon him till he felt annihilated, I now began to wonder if perhaps his observation might not be relevant to all the millions of ordinary people with the subjective bias towards life; was it not possible that they also partook of what Keats calls the "poetic character" [1] in a small way, but lacking the gift of utterance that goes to make a poet, they had never been able to come to understand themselves? If so, then the way out for them, the way out from their sense of inferiority and ineffectiveness, would surely be, not to seek to change their spots and turn themselves into men of power, but to concern themselves with the problem of knowing their own experience, with looking for forms for expressing what was happening to them. I do not mean that we should all try to join the ranks of minor poets or exhibit at local art shows—but that each of us should realize that the act of welding, by means of words or shape or musical sound or colour—into some sort of tangible form—a single moment of raw lived experience, is action as real and effective, though not as obviously so, as being able to order people about, break a sports record, be a social success, or whatever it is that most people with an "inferiority complex" wish so ardently that they could do. I realized how little reflective use averagely intelligent people can make of their own experience when I once tried to teach "psychology" to a class of adults drawn from various walks of life; what

[1] Whether the subjective bias towards life was part of what is usually called "the artistic temperament" I could not tell, for I did not know enough about artists; certainly I had met some who seemed to have entirely avoided the dangers of a misunderstood imagination; perhaps it was through the very fact of possessing gifts of sensory expression that they had never been tempted to wander into the Kingdom of the Trolls.

struck me most, apart from their enthusiasm for learning, was their fondness for arguing about abstractions, in contrast with their marked inability to say anything at all about the richness of their own varied day to day living.

I now began to see more clearly what Jung said about the special difficulties of the subjective temperament. For instance this tendency to accept for the moment the identity of whoever is with him, makes him tend also to accept their values; and since as Jung has said: "An extraverted consciousness is unable to believe in invisible forces," so the mere presence of the extraverted person makes him feel the whole foundation of his life wiped from under him. I began to observe examples of this, for instance, when merely listening to my friends talking at a party I would find that I had completely forgotten all the things I loved, the interests and views of those who were talking had become the only things that were real. I discovered also however that now, instead of being left after these occasions blindly depressed and resentful of the capacity of other people to impose their identity, I could accept their domination serenely; for I could know that afterwards, if I would only wait quietly, my own point of view would become clear again, I would even feel enriched by the previous submergence. Once after seeing *A Midsummer Night's Dream* I had wondered why the only lines that remained in my head were:

> "Contagious fogs; which, falling in the land,
> Have every pelting river made so proud,
> That they have overborne their continents."

Now however, I could see the bearing of this on my own discoveries, and also see how they pointed to a practical policy in planning leisure; for I must always allow time after such social contacts, recurrent periods of being alone in order to digest the experience, time for the flood of another personality to subside, or else I would find that the green corn had rotted and that:

"The fold stands empty in the drowned field."

Incidentally I now remembered that for years I had had a persistent dream of a tidal wave overwhelming a city. Since making these discoveries however, I had not had the dream again; instead I had dreamt of a whole series of tidal waves, and of myself happily surf-riding on the crest of each.

During these solitary times of digestion it was again through the emergence of an image that my own sense of identity returned. Often something would catch my eye, causing echoes through my whole body; just as I had once found that in foreign travel my mind had used strange sights and sounds as a means of giving tangible form to unexpressed impulses, so now I found I could deliberately produce analogous conditions at home. I could for instance, and I often did, go to the Zoo and wander round alone. I would find myself seeing all the animals in terms of moods, and find deep comfort in the sight of a lazy bear or the gusty angers of a gorilla. Even a sad chimpanzee was somehow comforting (see Fig. 4), though it was perhaps a salutary thought to reflect upon that one should find such a deep sense of affinity with chimpanzees and gorillas.

AN EXPERIMENT IN LEISURE

One day I wandered into the Insect House. There, straight before me was a jar, and in it were huge centipedes, exactly the same as the one that I had seen two years before as an image within myself. I stood quite still in front of the jar, feeling very sick, and waited. I felt as if I had swallowed the centipede and that the sickness was an attempt to get rid of it. Then quite

FIG. 4

absurdly, I found myself thinking of the digestive processes of owls, how in the country I had often found their casts, little bundles of claws and fur and bones. I remembered how the owl swallows his dinner whole, spewing up the indigestible bits that might otherwise tear his guts out, spewing them up at leisure in neat little bundles. Then I remembered too, how I had for days been blindly fighting the thought of someone who had criticized me, cruelly as I felt it, a cold-hearted tearing criticism that seemed to destroy my whole way of life—a poisonous centipede. And I had blindly tried to ecsape from it, forget it, vomit it out of me undigested. But now the feelings aroused by the sight of this centipede in the Zoo had given me a picture of what I was doing, so I deliberately held the criticism in my thoughts, just as I had deliberately stood and watched the centipede. And after this I found that the work which had been criticized expanded and became easier. I concluded that if one must be an owl as regards experience, swallowing it whole, not fastidiously tearing it and picking out the good meat, as an eagle does, and as most of my friends did, then one must also be content to wait for the process of digestion, not try to repudiate the whole thing because part of it seems hard and cutting.

There was another kind of solitary activity that I found very refreshing, though before this experiment I had always felt slightly guilty about it, for it seemed so egocentric. After a variety of social contacts I often felt so obsessed by them that I was reminded of the chameleon, who, according to the story, so takes the colour of his surroundings, that when placed upon a tartan, simply bursts. When feeling like this I would wander round the shops looking at clothes. In the look of some dress I would often find my lost sense of identity and a return to normal balance, with sufficient recuperation to be ready for work again.

Why awareness of one's own impulses should be so difficult for some temperaments was, I supposed, a matter for educationists—and psycho-analysts. Certainly education as I had experienced it had done very little to teach me how to know what I really wanted, but a great deal to lead me into accepting what other people wanted, while making believe that it was my own wish: in fact, it had been a very effective education in self-deception. But now, having found that one cannot live on pleasing other people and self-deception for ever, I had had to develop this technique for stalking impulses, as patiently and carefully as I had once stalked wild birds.

Once, for several days, I had found myself haunted by the name "Helios Hyperion". At first I had thought it was merely the sound of the words that I loved; but then I remembered how the followers of Odysseus had killed and eaten the sacred cattle of the sun because they were hungry, and that the disastrous contacts with storms and monsters of the sea were punishments for this profanity. So it occurred to me now that this effort to make sure what one loved, the method that I had tried to develop throughout this experiment, was tending the sacred cattle of the sun; and that to give up this effort, to accept what other people liked just for the sake of expediency,[1] as I so often did, not even aware that it was not my own likes, this was the profanity that laid one at the mercy of monstrous fears, Scylla and Charybdis, the continual false oppositions that haunt the path of the neurotic.

Of course I had to remind myself that this devotion

[1] After writing this book, I happened to read Sylvia Townsend Warner's *Lolly Willowes*. Delighted with it as literature, I was also interested to find the same witchcraft imagery that I had been driven to use in my own explorations; also the idea of a pact with the devil as necessary before certain temperaments can be what they need to be—rather than what other people want them to be.

to Helios Hyperion, this effort to make sure what one liked, must involve also the recognition of the fact that one could love darkness; otherwise, at any moment one might be whisked away to the gloomy underworld. And this recognition in oneself of desires not obviously "good", had another aspect, for I found that at moments a sense of satisfaction was growing which felt deeper and more stable than anything I had known— it was a sense of satisfaction that the facts were not as I wanted them. Once when having tea in Regent's Park on a Saturday afternoon, a little bored because we had not done anything more exciting, vaguely critical of the people round me, thinking how much more amusing a similar café in France would have been, suddenly my mood had changed, and I had become utterly glad for everything to be as it was; just because it was not what I had pictured, it had a newness that no mere realization of desire could possibly reach.

Expression, that I had felt to be the magical grip on the lion of desire, I now saw how it meant letting impulse and mood crystallize into outer form: not into purposive action determined by some outer goal, but expressive action determined by an inner vision—and this was the growing point, without which the subjective temperament remains stagnant and enwrapped in its own egoism. And the inescapable condition of true expression was the plunge into the abyss, the willingness to recognize that the moment of blankness and extinction was the moment of incipient fruitfulness, the moment without which the invisible forces within could not do their work. In other words, the person who is by nature dominated by the subjective factor is committed to a life of faith whether he likes it or not, since all his important mental processes are unconscious. But if he does not continually seek expression for his faith, for his sense of the force by which he is lived, then it remains, unknown to himself, in the infantile stage of domination by ogres and ravening beasts, and the false opposition of gods of light and the underworld; and his dependence upon the unseen within himself will be a continual torment.

CHAPTER SEVENTEEN

In trying to become clearer about the internal gesture of submission, another image now came into my mind, that useful fiction of perspective drawing which is called the vanishing point. It occurred to me that it is useless to argue what the vanishing point is, in itself it matters no more than the point on a horizon chosen by a sailor to direct his course, the only essential is that there be such points. Was it possible that it also did not matter what it was that I submitted to in my internal gesture, as long as I remembered to submit to something? My observations certainly pointed to the fact that you must trust in something, accept it, submit to it, not for moral reasons, but in order to let your mind function usefully at all. For without this reference to something beyond yourself you could never fully escape from that blind egocentric world of childhood in which truth tends to be simply what you would like to be true. I found myself continually remembering the two men in the Bible, the first who thanked God that he was not as other men are, the second who said "God be merciful to me a sinner". Before, I had always looked on this as a moral distinction, I had thought that the humble man was only "good", doing his duty, and therefore something that did not really concern me, as I had always thought that the idea of being good in the abstract, apart from practical benefits to people, was something I could not reach. But now I thought—'supposing this is nothing to do with being "good" or "bad", nothing to do with morals and "oughts", but a quite practical statement of fact about two different frames of mind?' Jesus said that the result of the humble state of mind was that the man felt "justified"; but I did not know what "justified" meant. What I did know, however, was that I could observe definite differences of result in myself from the two states of mind, even in the matter of ordinary perception of surroundings. For instance, I was one day driving over the mountain road to Granada in the spring, the cone-shaped, red-earthed foothills all covered with inter-lacing almond blossom. Also it was the first sunny weather after days of rain, so that I was filled with exultation as we climbed higher and higher into the clear mountain air. I was full of that kind of exulta-tion which makes one above oneself, I felt powerful and important, as if it was somehow my doing that the country was so lovely, or at least that I was cleverer than other people in having somehow got myself there to see it—I certainly felt thankful that I was not as other men are. Then I noticed that the character of the country was changing, so I began to try and fix something of what I had seen in words, or a plan for a sketch. But as soon as I tried to look back in my mind, I found there was nothing there, only the rather absurd memory of my own exultation, but no living vision at all of what had caused it. Then I remembered the pharisee and the publican, and began to say over and over, as if I were repeating a spell—"God be merciful to me a sinner". At once the look of the country was different, I was aware only of it, not of myself at all, and always afterwards it was that bit of Spain that I seemed to possess in imagination, whereas the earlier scenes I remembered only as something lost. After this I tried observing my everyday thoughts, and was shocked to find how often the pharasaical feeling cropped up; if Jesus meant that the humble state of mind was the condition of true imagination, no wonder I so often felt myself at the mercy of the other kind, the kind that is concerned, not with truth of experience, but with the magic satisfaction of personal desires.

The use of this idea of a perspective point had other practical results, I found it could be used to make one mind less when it was necessary to be away from people one loved. I found a note, written when I was forced to be away among strangers:

> ... at ... I missed D. very much, the uncomfortable feeling of self-completeness. At home I feel expanded, there is a polarity (I can see in my mind that diagram of the nucleus of one cell linked to that of another by radiating lines) I feel there lighter, more flowing, less heavy self-awareness, more alive. Here, except when alone or free to write, I'm like an encysted amoeba, cannot bear the weight of my own sense of self. But in the middle of this feeling I remembered You[1] and with that thought the heavy sense of self fell away.

---

[1] The sense of the "life by which one is lived" sometimes became so vivid that it seemed necessary to use a personal pronoun instead of an impersonal one.

AN EXPERIMENT IN LEISURE

I wondered whether it was not possible that this perspective point would also help one to grow out of the tendency to take the symbol for the fact, and the particular example of this tendency which is shown in over-possessiveness of people one loves. As long as your sense of the force that lives you is projected on to another person, then the continual presence of that person is utterly essential, you feel that the whole meaning of existence is with him, without him life has no significance whatever. In spite of the verdict of romantic literature and the films I was certain that such a state could only be a phase; one cannot live parasitically on another person's life for ever, eventually one must find and face the "other" in oneself, rather than in other people and their love for and dependence on oneself. And by a ritual submission to the perspective point, to an "other" which was not concrete material fact, I thought one did become less dependent on the concrete material signs of other peoples' affection, more able to allow them to have lives of their own, less fiercely possessive of their interest.

I thought that this finding of self in oneself was perhaps harder for a woman than a man. I had read: "The woman is always living in a condition of fusion with everything she knows, even when she is alone," [1] and though I did not believe it as a generalization I knew that it was true of me a good deal of the time. Further I read : " A man has a sense of his own personality for itself", but women "always get their sense of value from something outside themselves, from their

[1] *Sex & Character*, Otto Weininger, AMS Press Inc.

money and estates, the number and richness of their garments, the position of their box at the opera, their children, and, above all, their husbands or their lovers". In so far as this over-general statement contained a truth was it not perhaps the opposite side of the same picture to my sense of blankness and annihilation, that when the sense of self is a blankness there is a tendency to look for something to fill the blankness outside oneself, so that many women had potentially the "no identity" that Keats was so aware of, but quite unconsciously, not becoming aware of it and learning to trust its emptiness. This writer also says:

"Woman is the material on which man acts. No one misunderstands so thoroughly what a woman wants as he who tries to find out what is passing within her, endeavouring to share her feelings and hopes, her experiences and her real nature . . . Women are matter, which can assume any shape . . . Woman is nothing; therefore, and only therefore, she can become everything, whilst man can only remain what he is. A man can make what he likes of a woman; the most a woman can do is to help a man to achieve what he wants . . . Women have neither this nor that characteristic; their peculiarity consists in having no characteristic at all; the complexity and terrible mystery about women comes to this; it is this which makes them above and beyond man's understanding—man, who always wants to get at the heart of things . . .

"The meaning of woman is to be meaningless. She represents negation, the opposite pole from the Godhead, the other possibility of humanity. And nothing is so despicable as a man become female, and such a person will be regarded as the supreme criminal, even by himself. And so also is to be explained the deepest fear of man; the fear of woman, which is the fear of unconsciousness, the alluring abyss of annihilation.

"Women have no existence and no essence; they are not, they are nothing."

If for the word "woman" one read "the subjective temperament" then I thought these statements were very illuminating, particularly as a picture of the terror and hatred that an unrecognized tendency to subjectivity in oneself, whether man or woman, could arouse. But I wondered, was there really a tendency for women to be more subjective than men, for I knew a great many women who were as dominant and sure and interested in the visible as any man? I found an answer to this in the theory [1] that one must distinguish the subjective and objective bias on different levels, on the bodily level, on the emotional level, and on the level of understanding. It was pointed out to me that women were surely biassed towards subjectivity on the bodily level through the working of their reproductive glands, for the process of growing a baby is essentially subjective, after the moment of conception one merely had to let it happen, one could not direct and control its growth by purposes and planning. Also, since body and emotions are so closely connected, one would expect there would be an equally strong pull towards emotional subjectivity, towards submission and prostration before some god-like "other". But many women I knew managed to avoid this pull of the emotional submissiveness; they seemed to satisfy all their submissiveness in

---

[1] Elaborated by Theodore Faithfull.

their bodies so that their feelings were left free for the enjoyment of assertiveness, of gaiety and repartee and the power to control people by the attractiveness of their submissive bodies. For them life was comparatively easy, they had no inner struggles, they could say, "I've. always taken things as they come. It seems so obvious. One enjoys the pleasant things, avoids the nasty ones, There's nothing more to be said." On the other hand there were other women whose subjectivity, perhaps for some reason less fully satisfied in their bodies, was liable to sweep them into the sense of nothingness, into finding their whole life in something outside themselves.[1]

For them life was often difficult, for part of them resented this self-subjection, and wanted to preserve its own sense of identity intact. According to the theory, there seemed to be various possible ways out from this

---

[1] Of course to be completely identified with husband and children is in some ways an effective provision of Nature's, from the point of view of bringing up a family. But the trouble is that when the family has grown up and no longer needs you, the habit of knowing what you yourself want has almost become atrophied. So one tends still to live in the purposes of others, a process which is often very stifling to those others. I had often seen grown-up children coming to dread the hungry interest which a devoted mother showed in their purposes and affairs. Often I had heard it said, "If only mother would find some interest of her own!" But it is not so easy after twenty years or so of serving a continuous and imperious demand—unless, perhaps, you have discovered the trick of following up clues of your own little private enjoyments.

And of course, the same thing may happen to a man who has given the whole of himself to the practical purposes of his profession or business—when he retires, giving up the kind of life that is dominated by purpose, he is often reduced to the state of the larva in Capek's "Insect Play", who moans—"I'm so bo—red. I want—I want—I don't know what I want."

last conflict: the impulse to suffer, in the old sense of the word, that is to "allow" to "submit", this impulse could as it were slip down on to the bodily level, and there either "suffer" a baby to grow within one, or else cause one to suffer actual pain, to become ill. In both these cases a compromise is reached, submissiveness is satisfied, but also the sense of identity is preserved; for having a child can give a curious feeling of secure extension of one's being, while being ill is also a less reputable but sure way of insisting on one's existence. But I knew now that the impulse to suffer could also emerge in a third way—into the level of understanding—the sense of no identity could be recognized and accepted: instead of trying blindly to fill the emptiness with a picture of one's lover or one's possessions or one's children, one could recognize its emptiness, and somehow come to believe in that. And it was out of this suffering one's self to be lived by something not one's self that another creation came, the growth of forms of understanding.

But if this view of what happens were correct, how did it explain the undoubted fact that women have contributed very little towards the discovery of fresh aspects of experience? If they have this initial glandular bias towards subjectivity why are they not pre-eminently artists and poets? I found the following answer suggested: that because a woman can create with her body, it is infinitely harder for her to raise her subjectivity from the level of the body and mere lived experiences into the level of finding forms for her own experience. However much she may want to, the pull of the body is too strong for most women. But a man, being in any case unable to create within his own body, can bring the full force of his subjectivity, little or much, according to his temperament, to bear upon mental creation.

It now seemed to me that even some of my childhood games had been concerned with this same struggle. I remembered for instance:

'. . . at eleven or twelve, digging clay out of the garden, always making those clay pots and vases and trying to find the best way to fire them so that they would not crack . . . the joy when one morning, having buried my clay pot in the glowing ashes of the dying fire overnight, I now found the soft dirty brown clay changed to a lovely hard redness . . . and then, making a little triangular clay dish, like an ancient lamp, baking it till it was red, and one night in autumn filling it with dried herbs and rose leaves, and sitting all alone in the dark, cross-legged before it, I lit the herbs and watched the sweet-smelling smoke curl upwards. What a curious warmth of importance that memory has . . . and then that old black silk waistcoat that I filched from somewhere, and wore when we were playing Indians . . . I'd embroidered it with mysterious designs, and at the top of the back I put a bowl in red silk, with gold letters written across it—WAHONÉ—which meant MAGIC in the secret language we'd invented—curious that I put that bowl just over the part of my back where now I can feel most clearly the inner fact . . . and then that dish I found at a Charity Bazaar, a dish with mythical monsters on it—how I wanted it so badly that I went round to all the other stalls making them take back what I had bought, so that I should have enough money to buy the dish!'

Preoccupation with a magic cup, surely this was an obvious interest—a womb symbol. But was it the mother's womb, a yearning back to the magic dish of plenty, the effortless paradise, a theme which I knew now to be prominent in many psychological writings? Or was it a dim sense of the physical powers of the womb then growing with approaching adolescence? Or was it an intuition that, after passing through the fire, the pull of the physical womb could also become something else, that if I could accept the sense of myself as an empty cup then something else would grow out of the cup, something other than the bodily life that was just brown earth, clay from the garden? After my experience with the many-facedness of images, I thought that it meant all these things, and also that it expressed the blind struggle for a sense of identity and the various possible ways out: it foreshadowed the long struggle to develop an inner life that was not just an escape from reality, but the only means by which I could face it.

With this in mind I now remembered again the fairy tale I had written. The little old woman who was lame and lived alone in a remote suburb, this seemed to be a good picture of my feelings of inadequacy during adolescence, of being somehow remote from life and "not quite all there". In the story, the happy explorations of childhood had finished, the little fishes had been killed, cut up, and packed away in tins (ready for re-birth?). And they had been re-born in the adolescent, only at first as a vague restless questioning and bewildering impulse. I noticed now that it was by the help of a scientific expedition that the little old woman was able to follow up these mysterious impulses and finally achieve the deliberate annihilation which changed the face of her world. Was this a pictorial way of stating the fact that it was only by striving after the cold detached observation that science had shown me, that I had been at all able to discover the meaning of, and the means of satisfying, this restless urge, or escape from the sense of inadequacy which had in the past so haunted me? Then I remembered also the gong that the little old woman had had to make out of seven metals. This melting together of the seven metals, it seemed very like the welding together, by the fire of patient brooding concentration, of the different elements of experience. I also noticed now that the gong was shaped like a shield, and I found myself saying:

> "When thy song is shield and mirror
> To the fair snake-curlèd Pain,
> Where thou dar'st affront her terror
> That on her thou may'st attain
> Perséan conquest . . ."[1]

I thought it queer that I should remember these words, at this moment, when I had not thought of them at all for twenty years or more. But they were certainly apt, they well described the effect of anything powerful, people I was afraid of, or situations in which I thought something difficult was expected of me; these had cer-

[1] Francis Thompson.

tainly had a freezing effect on me all my life, producing a stony inability to feel anything at all. But all those years it had been action according to some standard, purposive action, that I had striven after: I had tried to kill fear with a sword instead of the mirror-shield that I had now found expression to be.

I remembered also that it was after all a woman who could not get her pig home from market, who could not make the dog bite, or the stick beat, or the fire burn, or the water quench, or the ox drink, or the butcher kill, or the rope hang, or the rat gnaw, or the cat kill, or the cow give milk, or the hay makers give hay—until she had gone to the stream and filled a bucket with water; water, and the empty bucket, the same symbols that Lao Tze so often used to describe that Simple Way of Life, which does not foster its own being.

There was another thing that I had noticed about childhood memories, particularly when looking through books that I had once loved: the memories seemed to be stirred up from one's blood and one's bones and the pit of one's stomach, not in one's head at all, as more recent memories seemed to be. But of course there were adult "blood and bones" feelings too. Someone had once quoted to me a translation of a Chinese poem, a verse-letter of a girl to her lover; it ended with—

"I desire that my bones be mingled with yours
For ever and for ever and for ever."

This feeling of the immortality of one's love, did not, I thought, refer to actual time, it existed just the same even if one was pretty certain from experience that the feeling was only temporary. But that it did mean something I was pretty sure. For I found the same feeling about certain pictures, a feeling of their existence beyond and outside time, and also sometimes in music, or in glimpses of people's faces. Someone had once said to me, when describing his way of living: "You see, I don't believe in immortality or anything of that sort, so I just do as I like." But I thought that if you really trouble to find out what you like there is an immortality of here and now that is utterly different from the fear of punishment or hope of reward in after life. So it seemed to me now that that state which was somehow forced upon one by falling in love with a person, was also a state that could be brought about deliberately, brought about by taking up into the glow of brooding consciousness the images of the blood and the bones; and in so far as one did this, one was no longer at the mercy of the misunderstandings of the past, one's past became one's own to use, not a litter of misconceptions tripping up one's every step.

SUMMING UP

I DID not know how far any of this account might be important for other people, or whether what I found only grew out of a special idiosyncrasy of temperament. But I thought it possible that others might at least gain something from the use of the method, even though it is probable that their findings would be quite different. For to know where your impulses are taking you is surely useful, not only in the management of private life, but also in one's attitude to public affairs. We are continually reading of how democracy demands that all of us should think more clearly, reason more adequately, about public affairs. But also, it has in recent years been proved that the inborn reasoning capacity of the majority of us is not very high. I wondered whether the problem of the education of opinion towards public affairs might not be approached from a different angle; instead of trying to teach people to reason better, which is very likely beyond the inborn capacity of most of us, why not teach us to understand our feelings better, to know what we really want, so that we would be less at the mercy of unscrupulous exploiters who like to rush us into what suits them? Also, many psychologists say that it is the thwarting of impulse that makes people aggressive, long years of never being able to do what they want or have what they

220

want, thwartings that began in earliest childhood with the prohibitions and compulsions of social living. But it is obviously not only external compulsions that thwart people, it is also the difficulty of knowing what they want even when it is within their power to get it. So even when they do get leisure and money and the external freedom that money brings, they often do not know what to do with it. Certainly education might be less concerned with teaching children how to reproduce information and make a show of reasoning that has no basis in their own real experience, and more with teaching them how to know what they want, how to be alert to the changing seasons of inner need. But I did not think this alertness would come by simply turning them loose to "do as they like", without the guidance and protection of a tradition. For it seemed to me, after this experiment, that knowing what you really want is an exceedingly delicate process: to bridge the gap between vague inner urgencies and the practical possibilities of the outer world requires the finest co-ordination and economy of mental power.

Since living is such a complicated business, it was of course very difficult to prove whether any of the changes I observed were definitely the result of the method I had adopted. All I could say was that my mind had produced the images I have attempted to describe, in answer to the question—"What do I find most interesting?" and I had also gained some idea of the kind of interferences at work in the matter of leisure. And whether as a result of this method or not, it seemed to me that I had also found out how to experience more fully, how to get closer in touch with what was going on around as well as inside me. I had discovered that, not through deliberate reasoning, logic, argument, but by another process that I can only call "image-finding", I could come closer in touch with the movement of life. And it was this process, rather than logic and reasoning, that seemed actually to have made it more possible for me to live reasonably. By living more reasonably I meant, a little less liable to strive for incompatible ends, less liable to impose unnecessary duties upon myself and then be miserable about it, less liable to look round for other people of whom I could say that all my inadequacies were their fault, less liable to that most uncomfortable state of wanting to grab other people's successes for oneself. To wait quietly and watch for images, for those pictures and metaphors that the mind itself threw up, this seemed to be the way that understanding grew —if only I could remember to do it—the way to escape from the glib ping-pong of argument, from knowing in theory what ought to be done but not being able to do it, from the divorce between thought and action, from sterile intellectuality.

The discovery of the power of these half-pictured ideas that drew me like a magnet had certainly been surprising. I had been so bred up in the belief in argument and purposes that this other way of living seemed impossibly vague and spineless. Also I had often been filled with a kind of horror to observe how the opinions of groups of people could be stampeded by an image, particularly an image with the word "red" attached. But now that I had discovered more about the nature of images I was not so surprised at their power. For I had learnt that it was in these images that unrecognized desires expressed themselves, that when people purported to be talking of external facts, but talked with extreme enthusiasm or extreme hatred, then what they said had less reference to the facts than to their own inner needs. I had been most shocked when I found that some of those images which had seemed to grow out of my most intimate and private experience, and that I had thought represented for me the kernel of the problem of escape from the narrow focus of egoism, were being used by others to foster what seemed to me that most sinister form of egoism—jingoistic nationalism. For I had read in the newspapers that pagan rituals were being revived in Germany, as part of the movement to glorify violence and to discredit the teachings of Christ. When I first read this I had been tempted to throw over my whole enterprise, I thought that all this time I must have been following after a will-o'-the-wisp, that images in their double-facedness were false gods after all. But gradually I had come to see another possible explanation.

In a review of a book which expounded the racial beliefs of Nazi Germany I read:

". . . Passions and prejudices notoriously prevent men from thinking clearly and acting justly. For the last two or three thousand years moralists and philosophers have told us that we ought to make efforts to overcome our passions and discount our prejudices. Modern nationalists are of an opposite opinion. The attempt to replace passion and prejudice by reason is absurd and even wicked;

for each nation's passions and prejudices are in reality its own peculiar brand of reason." [1]

The phrase "the attempt to replace passion and prejudice by reason" struck me particularly. If that was what moralists and philosophers had been trying to do for the last two or three thousand years was it not perhaps time to ask why they had so little succeeded, and whether it might not be that they had been using the wrong method? Was it not possible that Freud was right, and that man's discovery of reason had, so to speak, gone to his head, with the result that many reformers assumed it should be possible to make everybody live by reason all the time, when actually the great majority of people can never live by reason, but only by habit and by faith? It was obvious that among even the professionally intelligent, they were only intelligent over a small range of problems, you could always find subjects in which they had none of the open-mindedness which reason demands. And even those who talked reasonably so often acted unreasonably, there was this great gap between what people knew would be sensible to do and what they did do. Reason and passion were notoriously so utterly unlike—and yet people seemed to assume that the transition from one to the other, as a guiding force in living, could be accomplished in a single bound. It seemed obvious to me now, that there must be a mediator between them; then I discovered that Jung had said, of the mythological type of image, that it has the capacity to reconcile idea with feeling, to appear "in the rôle of media-

[1] Aldous Huxley in the *New Statesman*.

tor, once again proving its redeeming efficacy, a power it has always possessed in the various religions".[1] But if this were true, and it certainly seemed borne out by my own experience, who were the manipulators of images in public life? In democratic countries the most powerful manipulators of vital images seemed to be the film-producers, the advertisers and the popular press; and these on the whole manipulated them quite irresponsibly for their own financial advantage, though at times of national stress and in elections they were also used politically. Under dictatorships vital images seemed used more deliberately for political purposes, primitive images of blood-brotherhood, of blood sacrifice for one's country, of an absolute father-god-dictator at the head of the nation.

I could not doubt now that such notions were effective in controlling a people's mood; what worried me, however, was when they were taken literally. My own experience seemed to show that such images were really outward and visible signs of inward experience, and I thought that their power in controlling mood must lie in the fact that, unlike abstract ideas and reasoning, their outwardness was deeply rooted in simple sensation, in the concreteness of colour and shape and texture and sound and movement. Yet this very source of their power was also the source of their danger; for because of the great difficulty that every child had, and man had had in his growth from childhood, in recognizing that thoughts have a separate kind of existence from things, the double meaning of the image so easily

[1] Jung: *Psychological Types*, p. 559.

225

got lost, the whole matter got transferred into the outside world. Instead of vehicles for the communication of inner private immediate experience, they had been taken as real in their own right, because to believe in the innerness of experience was difficult, but to cling to a concrete statement of apparent external fact was easy. The whole history of popular religions could I thought be looked upon as a materialization of the image; and once it was no longer looked on as a truth of spirit, but instead a truth of external fact, then it became the instrument of all kinds of exploitation—lustful, political, social, the instrument of the crudest infantile desire to be king of the castle and to prove that others are dirty rascals. But the fact that they could be so exploited did not take away from the truth of images in terms of internal experience. The fact that dictators had realized the power of images for political purposes in controlling and unifying a nation need not make me discard my own discovery that they had power to unify my own chaos of experience. Neither need I let the knowledge that newspapers give sordid details of trunk murders simply in order to increase their sales deter me from recognizing the fact that these images had a definite meaning for me. (Incidentally after writing this book, I found I was no longer particularly interested in trunk murders.)   Nor could I any longer scoff, as I had sometimes been tempted to do, at the power of images over other people, or at the spectacle of thousands of essentially normal people flocking enthusiastically to see, for instance, the external trappings of their image of kingship.

SUMMING UP

From all this it was hard to avoid the conclusion that by taking notice of those feelings and images that seemed to be in my blood and bones rather than in my head, I had found myself able to behave, not less reasonably, but more so. Apparently it was as much a false extreme to try and live by reason alone, leaving the passions out of count, as to ignore reason and put passion in its place as the guiding force of life. For myself at least, I was sure that the way to pass safely between this Scylla and Charybdis was to listen to the voice of the blood and the bones, but not to make the mistake of taking it at its face value, not to take its images literally and assume that it was talking about external truth when in fact it was talking about inner truth, about the problem of the inner organization of desire and experience. For if you lived recognizing only the outer half of the facts, taking images literally, as many people did, then the ignored inner facts, the demands of the inner organization of desire, took their revenge by distorting your external vision, and you would read with gusto the lies of atrocity-mongers and pass them on to your friends as if they were external truth.

And the way to ensure that I would use these images in the service of truth of experience rather than as bogus pictures of external fact seemed to be the repeated ritual gesture of giving up my private desires. This seemed to be my answer to the question of whether the feeling of importance about any idea could ever be trusted.

The fact that the mere repetition of such words as

227

"I am nothing, I have nothing, I want nothing" should have definite mental effects did not surprise me, since experiments in auto-suggestion have frequently shown the power of a mere phrase. Also there seemed to be other theoretical grounds for such a gesture being effective. It seemed likely that a person who is by temperament inclined to look inward, and who is therefore susceptible to the power of the image and the idea, was particularly at the mercy of ideas of himself. He particularly minded what people thought of him, since to him ideas were real and powerful things, whether in his own mind or in other people's. To the outward looking person, the practical man of action who had never felt the full power of the idea, perhaps the inner gesture of renunciation was unnecessary—or quite incomprehensible. But for the inward turning person the imagined pictures of himself were, I felt sure, a perpetual entanglement, preventing him being what he needed to be. I remembered Ibsen's portrayal in *The Wild Duck* of the unsuccessful inventor, whose life consisted entirely in fashioning images of himself and admiring them; and I thought of other Ibsen characters, who all seemed to be struggling with the power of the idea: Hedda Gabbler, also obsessed by particular pictures of herself which make the contrast with reality intolerable —the Master Builder, so full of the power of the idea that he feels others are compelled to action by his unspoken wish. Incidentally I remembered that the creative life of the Master Builder had begun with a fire, and I have already shown how often fire images had been associated in my own mind with a sense of freeing of the imagination from personal desire.[1] And then there was Hamlet, who had been apparently sufficiently successful as a man of action, but who also suffered from the power of the idea and had become spellbound by it. Was not Shakespeare saying that the laws of the imagination are not the same as the laws of action, that you cannot escape the domination of an evil image by deliberate contriving towards a purpose, you can only escape it by renouncing all purposes and becoming aware of the dominating image? And you cannot become aware of it, that is, know part of yourself, without momentarily at least renouncing all preconceived pictures of yourself, knowing nothing, having nothing, wanting nothing—"the readiness is all"?

There was another possible explanation of the apparent effect of the gesture. Before this experiment I had found much of Freudian theory so difficult to grasp that I had given up the attempt to read it. Now, however, I had ventured to study it again, and (from a book

[1] I felt there were many more clues to be found in Ibsen's plays, for he seemed so often preoccupied with the various aspects of this same problem. The doctor in "The Wild Duck" insists on the need for a vital fantasy to help people get through their lives; and yet in other characters the effect of destructive fantasies is so often shown. And the Master Builder, whose dreams had become so constructive and concretely expressed in "homes for human beings", is finally destroyed by the power fantasies of a romantic girl. Also the fear of falling from the tower and the fear of competition from the younger generation that continually haunted him, both these seemed to indicate Ibsen's concern with the same problem that was the main theme of "Within the Gates", the intimations of mortality which seem to haunt the path of the potentially creative temperament. Perhaps then the fall from the tower, which the girl greeted with such a note of triumph, was really a triumph, a triumph of acceptance.

written for laymen [1]) found that I could at last relate it to my own experience, for much of it explained the spontaneous images I had been observing in myself. For instance, I read:

> "It may happen that you have sufficient self-awareness to know something of how painful it is to realize that one hates a person whom one loves, and has impulses of rage and destruction against those whom one also values and treasures and desires above all else. It is an intensely depressing truth to have to face. The pain is hardly to be borne, and it has to be lessened or got rid of by some means. For the little child, this is the nodal problem of his whole development . . .
>
> "The 'bad' mother is the mother that he rages against in his fury, and wants to destroy because she cannot satisfy him in the moment of demand. The 'good' mother is she who feeds and tends and loves and makes him secure." [2]

This certainly seemed a likely origin for the 'Dis-Adonis' conflict of my fairy tale, and also for the conflict between the Inner Fact that was good, and the poisonous centipede; for I read also that the child "in his fantasy . . . takes into himself everything which he perceives in the outside world".[3]   But I also gathered that the Freudian made much of the idea that an impulse towards suffering was a self-punishment for one's own 'badness', an attempt even to destroy oneself because of the terror of one's own childish destructive impulses against people who thwarted one's appetites. This would certainly be one explanation of satisfaction achieved in a sense of being destroyed by an alien

---

[1] *On the Bringing Up of Children*, by Five Psycho-Analysts.
[2] Susan Isaacs.   [3] Melanie Klein.

force, and the sense of peace achieved by this ultimate submission; for in these terms one had simply given up the moral struggle, in giving up one's identity one had also given up the responsibility. I found that these Freudians recognized even the wish to die to be often a sort of propitiation, a sacrifice that would 'make good' the evil that one had done in secret thoughts, in wishing to possess and destroy. Perhaps they were right and this really was the primitive basis of it all; or perhaps Groddeck was right in believing that the desire to suffer was as innate as the desire to hurt, and was, in its origin, an essential part of the process of physical creation, the moral struggle that the Freudians describe being only a secondary elaboration. But in any case, neither explanation ruled out the possibility that this same impulse could be used constructively, in fact must be so used by certain temperaments: they must periodically go through the Valley of Humiliation, must deliberately lose the sense of their own identity, must watchfully let themselves be possessed and fertilized by experience, if they are to achieve any real psychic growth.

I also found a hint of the use of my internal gesture in certain discussions about the difficulties of thinking, hints which confirmed my guess that the gesture of inner poverty was not merely a matter for sermons and piety, but an essential part of the everyday task of learning how to live reasonably. I read for instance of the kind of logical fallacies all of us are liable to, and the disastrous effects of desire determining opinion. But I had not yet found any instruction that was intel-

231

ligible to me of how to avoid these pitfalls. Then one day I read: "The opposite of thinking clearly is being muddled. To be conscious of being muddled is a horrible experience. To avoid it we may even be tempted to shut our minds and swallow a belief, ready-made, from some expert authority."[1] This made me wonder, if it were true that false thinking comes even partly from the horrible experience of being muddled, then would not one way out be to learn how to accept the experience of being muddled? I knew only too well how strong was the impulse to be certain, to lay down the law, to have things in black and white. But my mind had now driven me on to become aware of this other mood, the acceptance of emptiness, and to discover that whenever one achieved this there was then no need to force one's thinking into a misleading clarity. And certainly it was only then when I had given up all striving after it that I ever achieved any clarity, though unfortunately not often even then.

There seemed to be another result of this experiment. Psychologists said that psychic health required, not only that one should learn to face the facts, but also that one should learn to be independent, not to be continually seeking protection and someone to rely upon. Just as I had often been aware of the tendency in myself to run away from the facts, moods of continually hankering after something different, so also I had been aware of the desire to find someone I could rely on; I had often found myself deeply resentful when I was forced to

[1] L. Susan Stebbing: "Imagination and Thinking," pamphlet published by the British Institute of Adult Education.

admit that someone I liked was not a paragon of all the virtues. I had known this was stupid, but I had not known how to stop myself doing it: I had found I could not come nearer maturity by an act of will, or even by taking thought, if taking thought meant argument with oneself. But now, having discovered the possibility of submitting oneself, in recurrent moments, to an inner fact instead of an outer one, I found myself quite able to admit that no one was perfect, however much I might love them; I seemed to be freed from the restless search for the ideal person, the perfect leader. I could now quite happily face the fact that there was no one I had ever met who could be trusted to be always right, whereas before this knowledge had made me miserable. It certainly did seem that the lust for security and sub-mission, a primitive instinct which was undoubtedly imperious and strong, could be more safely turned to-wards something within, whether you called it your fate or your daemon or your God; for to let it find its expression in a blind external slavery would leave you totally at the mercy of chance and circumstance. My conclusion was that there was a psychological necessity to pay deliberate homage to something, since if it is not deliberate it will be furtive, but none the less powerful and at the mercy of public exploiters of furtive emo-tion—the politicians, the atrocity-mongers, the popular press; and also the psychological necessity to find your own pantheon of vital images, a mythology of one's own, not the reach-me-down mass-produced mythology of Hollywood, of the newspapers, or the propaganda of dictators.

AN EXPERIMENT IN LEISURE

Someone has said: "Those who can, do. Those who can't, teach." I might have added: "Those who can't, write." Probably there are a great many people in the world who have always known what I have been laboriously discovering, people who simply live it in their daily lives, and do not need to write about it because they can do it. But even if it is true that the fact of writing about a certain activity implies that one is not very good at doing it, this does not free one from the need to write, it is not much good refusing crutches when you have broken your leg just because most people have two good feet to walk upon.

I had found repeatedly that once a thing was said, in matters of feeling, then it was no longer true. Because of this there can be no real conclusion to this book. Having tried as far as I was able, and very confusedly, to make a clear statement, I knew I must now let it go and feel as if I had never even started. Once in adolescence, I had written some poems and shown them to my father. He said: "Go on writing but always tear up what you have written." Disappointed, for I was rather proud of the poems, I did not tear them up, but also I never tried to write any more poetry. But now I knew that the fact of the inadequacy of any expression was only a reason for trying again, like the importunate widow, not for stopping. And here I remembered Christian in the castle of Giant Despair. Once I had written:

> . . . doubt, what does that mean? Something utterly destructive, the refusal to do something because you cannot see the end of it, refusal to go on in the dark? The

Giant tried to make them commit suicide, is it the refusal to leap beyond what you can see at the moment, for instance, to refuse to write or draw or paint even though you have no certainty of what will come?   But in the middle of it all Christian remembers that he has a key, isn't that true, how utterly one forgets one's discoveries . . .

I knew also that a perpetual difficulty preventing one sticking to the problem of expression was that "all or noneness" of blind thinking, that I had discovered in my first enterprise.[1]   To the infantile part of one's mind everything that was not a world-shattering success was an utter failure, so that as soon as the lameness of one's attempt to express the fiery vision was apparent, then there was an irresistible impulse to give up the whole thing as hopeless.   But just in so far as I refused to give up, so I found experience becoming continually richer: experience, this thing which was always more than all that could be said about it—and yet in order to know it, you had to be continually trying to say things about it.

[1] *A Life of One's Own.*